The QSBS Playbook

How Section 1202 Lets Founders and Angel Investors Exclude Millions in Capital Gains Under the Expanded 2025 Rules

Patricia M. Ashworth

Published by NobleTrex Press

For permissions and other inquiries, write to:

P.O. Box 3132, Framingham, MA 01701, USA

Contents

Introduction

Imagine two founders, Sarah and Marcus, who are celebrating on the exact same Tuesday. They are entirely unacquainted, living in different cities, operating in different industries, but they share a phenomenal milestone: they have both just sold their startup for exactly $15 million in cash. They have poured five grueling years into their respective companies. They have missed birthdays, survived near-bankruptcies, and staked their financial lives on a vision that finally paid off. On paper, they are identical success stories.

But when tax season rolls around, their realities aggressively diverge.

Marcus hands his paperwork over to his CPA and receives a stomach-dropping reality check. Between federal capital gains taxes, the Net Investment Income Tax, and his state tax bill, Marcus owes the government somewhere in the neighborhood of $4 million. He signs a check that could have bought an island, severely downgrading the life-changing nature of his exit.

Sarah also hands her paperwork to her CPA. A few days later, she gets her return. Her federal tax liability on that $15 million windfall? Zero dollars. Not a single cent. She keeps the entire amount, minus a minor state tax obligation, effectively walking away with millions of dollars more than Marcus for building a company of the exact same value.

Sarah didn't funnel her money through a shadowy Cayman Islands shell corporation. She didn't employ an army of aggressive offshore tax attorneys, and she didn't exploit a legally dubious gray area. In fact, the IRS was completely aware of what she was doing and enthusiastically blessed the entire transaction.

The only difference between Sarah and Marcus came down to a few seemingly mundane administrative decisions made years earlier—decisions about entity type, issuance timing, and equity structure. Sarah had accidentally, or perhaps deliberately, activated Section 1202 of the Internal Revenue Code, commonly known as the Qualified Small Business Stock (QSBS) exclusion. Marcus had not.

If you have never heard of QSBS, or if you only know it as a vague acronym tossed around on venture capital podcasts, prepare to permanently change the way you view startup equity.

Section 1202 is not a loophole. "Loophole" implies an unintended error in the law that taxpayers are sneakily exploiting. QSBS is the exact opposite. It is a giant, neon billboard erected by the federal government, attempting to bribe you into taking enormous financial risks. The government knows that early-stage startups are the engine of job creation and technological dominance. But they also know that investing in or founding a startup is statistically a terrible idea, prone to failure and total loss of capital. To balance the scales, Congress wrote a provision into the tax code: if you put your time, money, or talent into a qualified domestic C corporation, and you hold onto that stock for the required period, you can exclude up to 100 percent of your capital gains from federal taxes when you finally sell.

Historically, this exclusion was capped at $10 million, or ten times your original basis in the stock, whichever was greater. It required a strict, unbroken five-year holding period. If you sold at four years and three hundred and sixty-four days, the IRS handed you a devastating tax bill. It was a harsh, all-or-nothing cliff that forced founders to reject perfectly good acquisition offers just to run down the clock.

But the game has fundamentally changed. Under the expanded 2025 rules—ushered in by recent legislative adjustments—the landscape of startup taxation has been blown wide open. The rigid five-year cliff has been replaced by a tiered holding period schedule, allowing partial exclusions for exits at three and four years. The overall dollar cap has been dramatically increased to $15 million for qualifying new stock, and the gross-assets threshold for a company to even be considered a "small business" has been bumped to $75 million.

These changes have transformed QSBS from a rigid, niche tax benefit into the single most powerful wealth-creation tool available to the modern entrepreneur, angel investor, and early startup employee. The expanded rules mean more companies qualify, more exits are protected, and more people can shelter generation-altering amounts of money from the IRS.

Yet, despite the staggering amounts of money on the table, the startup ecosystem is littered with tragic stories of blown QSBS exclusions.

The tax code does not hand you $15 million in tax-free money just because you feel you deserve it. Section 1202 is an unforgiving obstacle course of technical requirements. It demands that you acquire the stock at "original issuance," meaning you generally cannot buy it from another founder. It requires the company to operate an "active" and "qualified" business, intentionally shutting out consultants, lawyers, and certain financial firms. It mandates that you hold actual stock—not unexercised options, not unconverted SAFEs, and not convertible notes.

Every single day, brilliant founders inadvertently destroy their QSBS eligibility because they form an LLC to pass through early losses, converting to a C corporation entirely too late. Every day, early engineers lose out on millions because they sit on unexercised stock options, fundamentally misunderstanding when their holding period actually begins. Every day, angel investors blindly agree to stock redemptions or secondary sales that trigger a hidden legal trap, mathematically erasing their tax benefits overnight.

They only discover the mistake at the finish line. When an acquisition is looming, the due diligence teams descend, the tax advisors are called in, and the cap table is scrutinized. It is in these final, exhausted moments of a deal that someone realizes the paperwork was signed on the wrong date, or the entity was structured incorrectly, or a seemingly harmless share buyback tainted the entire cap table. There is no worse feeling in the financial world than sitting in a lawyer's office, staring at a multi-million-dollar exit, and realizing you will lose a third of it to the government because of a careless paperwork error made four years ago.

You cannot afford to learn about QSBS at the end of your startup experience. You must understand it at the beginning, monitor it in the middle, and aggressively protect it at the exit.

The playbook you are holding is engineered to solve this exact problem. It is designed to bridge the massive gap between the dense, impenetrable language of the tax code and the practical, everyday reality of building and funding companies. Whether you are a first-time founder bootstrapping in your garage, an early employee staring at an intimidating equity compensation package, an angel investor writing a $25,000 check, or a serial entrepreneur looking to maximize your next venture, you have a distinct role to play in the QSBS ecosystem.

To master this environment, you do not need to become a tax attorney, but you do need a practical command of the mechanics that drive gain calculation and eligibility. We will start by stripping away the jargon surrounding capital gains, basis, and equity. You will learn exactly why the distinction between a SAFE, a warrant, an option, and restricted stock is not just legal trivia, but the very mechanism that dictates whether you pay millions in taxes or nothing at all.

From there, we will deconstruct the core rules of Section 1202 into a ruthless, actionable checklist. You will learn precisely who qualifies, what original issuance really means in practice, and how to monitor your company's assets and activities to ensure you never cross the invisible lines that disqualify your business. We will dissect the catastrophic consequences of poorly timed share redemptions, teaching you how to avoid the midstream mistakes that quietly poison an otherwise healthy cap table.

With the baseline established, we will apply the accelerant: the expanded 2025 rules. You will discover how the date your shares are issued now fundamentally dictates which tax regime you operate under. We will explore the strategic implications of the new three- and four-year holding period tiers, allowing you to confidently evaluate early M&A offers without the paralyzing fear of the old five-year cliff. We will break down how the increased $15 million cap and the $75 million asset threshold widen your planning horizon, turning QSBS from a passive hope into a proactive strategy.

But understanding the rules is only half the battle; the real value is in optimization. Once you know how QSBS works, you can legally and ethically maximize its limits. You will learn how founders use 83(b) elections to anchor their tax basis at zero while starting their holding period clock immediately. You will see how early employees can strategically time their option exercises to separate their equity into distinctly taxed tranches. Most importantly, you will learn the art of "stacking"—how smart investors and founders use trusts, family transfers, and pass-through entities to multiply that $15 million limitation, potentially shielding $30 million, $45 million, or even more from federal capital gains.

Of course, a brilliant tax strategy on a spreadsheet is utterly useless if it falls apart in the real world. A company exit is a chaotic, high-stress event where acquiring companies care about their own liability, not your tax bill. You will be guided through the harsh realities of exits, rollover options, and federal reporting. If you are forced to sell before your holding period is met, you will learn how Section 1045 allows you to take your tax-free gains and roll them directly into a new startup, keeping your money entirely out of the IRS's reach. We will also confront the frustrating reality of state taxes, ensuring you understand exactly which states respect the federal QSBS rules and which ones will demand their cut regardless.

Finally, because the best offense is a good defense, we will autopsy the most common ways people accidentally destroy their QSBS eligibility. By examining real-world formation mistakes, operational drift, and documentation gaps, you will develop a risk-management mindset. You will know exactly which documents to save, which board approvals to demand, and how to build a bulletproof substantiation file that will survive the most aggressive IRS audit or buyer due diligence.

Let's be brutally honest for a moment. You are going to spend the next several years working impossibly hard. If you are a founder, you are going to trade your sleep, your peace of mind, and your youth for the chance to build something extraordinary. If you are an investor, you are going to risk hard-earned capital on ideas that most people think are crazy. If you are an early employee, you are going to accept a below-market salary in exchange for the promise of equity upside.

You are taking all the risk. Do not fumble the reward at the one-yard line because you didn't understand the tax code.

The rules of wealth creation in the private markets are entirely written in the language of equity and taxes. Those who understand this language get to keep the wealth they build. Those who ignore it end up working for the government. The millions of dollars in tax savings currently sitting inside Section 1202 belong to whoever is organized enough to claim them.

It is time to turn the page, protect your equity, and ensure that when your exit day finally arrives, you keep exactly what you have earned.

Chapter 1

Why QSBS Matters and How the Playbook Works

Most tax rules feel like fine print. QSBS is different: one early decision about how you receive, hold, or transfer startup stock can echo all the way to a future sale and mean the difference between an ordinary tax bill and excluding millions in gain. This chapter shows why the stakes are so high and how to read the rest of the playbook with the right questions in mind.

1.1 Section 1202 in Plain English

Think of Section 1202 as a deal the government offers you *only if you keep your side of the bargain*. You take the high-risk bet of owning stock in a young company early. If the stock is the right *kind* of stock, the company stays the right *kind* of company, and you hold it the right *way* for long enough, the tax law may let you erase a big chunk of the capital gains you'd otherwise owe when you sell.

That's the emotional truth of QSBS: it can turn a life-changing exit from a tax event into something closer to a clean win. But it does it with a very particular personality. QSBS isn't the sort of tax benefit that politely asks for a few documents at the end. It's more like a picky bouncer who decides, years later, whether you were on the list the whole time.

The hard part is that nothing about startup life feels built for that level of slow, legalistic consistency. Startups are improvisation: pivots, financings, side deals, employee departures, secondary sales, buybacks, SAFE conversions, and "we'll paper it later." QSBS is the opposite. QSBS rewards the people who treat equity like a long-term asset with a paper trail, not a sentimental trophy sitting in a cap table.

What makes QSBS surprisingly simple is the basic story. What makes it dangerous is the number of ways the story can stop being true.

QSBS is a three-part story, not a single label

The fastest way to keep QSBS in your head—without turning your brain into a tax outline—is to treat it as three moving parts that all have to stay aligned:

- *The stock*: how you got it and what, exactly, it is.
- *The company*: what the business is and whether it stays within the lines.
- *The shareholder*: who owns it (legally), and whether they're an eligible type of owner.

That's it. Not in the sense that it's easy—but in the sense that nearly every QSBS "surprise" at exit traces back to one of those three parts quietly drifting out of alignment years earlier.

Here's the trick: in everyday startup conversation, people talk about "having equity," "being on the cap table," or "owning a piece." QSBS cares about the legal edges of that ownership. The difference between *stock you received from the company* and *stock you bought from someone else* can be the difference between tax-free gain and fully taxable gain. The difference between stock held in your name and stock held through an entity can change who gets the benefit. The difference between a company that's "basically a software startup" and a company that's "basically selling the founders'expertise" can matter more than the pitch deck.

If you want a plain-English job description for QSBS planning, it's this: *keep those three parts boringly consistent while everything else changes.*

How QSBS shows up in real life: three familiar characters

QSBS doesn't arrive with a marching band. It usually sneaks into your life through one of three very normal startup moments: formation stock, early option exercises, or a first check.

1) The founder who buys common at formation

A founder often starts with the cleanest QSBS setup in the whole ecosystem: a purchase of common stock directly from the company when the company is tiny. The purchase price is usually tiny too—sometimes fractions of a cent per share. That low price becomes your *basis* (your starting "tax investment" for measuring gain later). If the company grows into something huge, the gain can be enormous, which makes QSBS potentially enormous.

The founder's temptation is also classic: treat the early equity issuance as "done" once the incorporation documents are signed. But QSBS doesn't care that you meant well at formation. It cares about what the company becomes, what it owns, what it does, and how it handles its stock.

Founders are uniquely exposed to QSBS problems because they're the people who can accidentally create them. A buyback to clean up a messy cap table. A redemption to help a departing cofounder. A "quick fix" to solve a financing complication. A choice about entity structure or conversions. These can all be rational business decisions and still be QSBS-hostile if handled casually.

The founder advantage is control. The founder risk is also control.

2) The early employee who exercises options (or doesn't)

Employees experience QSBS less like a single clean event and more like a series of time-based doors:

- When the option is granted, the clock usually *hasn't* started for QSBS.
- When the option is exercised and you actually acquire stock, the clock typically *starts.*
- If you leave, you may have a short window to exercise—or lose the ability to buy the shares at all.

That timeline creates a very employee-specific kind of regret: the person who helped build a company early, watched it grow, and then realizes their QSBS holding period started later than they assumed—or never started—because they waited to exercise.

The employee trap isn't stupidity; it's normal human behavior under financial pressure. Exercising costs money. Exercising creates paperwork. Exercising may create tax consequences even before there's liquidity. And yet the difference between exercising early and exercising late can be the difference between qualifying under a favorable holding period and missing it by months or years.

A second employee trap is assuming the company will "handle QSBS." Companies don't get QSBS. *Shareholders* do. The company can make it easier or harder, but the benefit lands on your personal return. That means you, the employee, need your own record of what you acquired, when you acquired it, and how.

3) The angel who writes the first check

Angels tend to think in rounds, terms, and outcomes. QSBS forces one more question into the mix: *am I buying from the company or from someone else?*

When an angel buys newly issued stock directly from the company, they're typically in the zone QSBS was built for: early risk capital going into a small operating business. When an angel buys in a secondary transaction—purchasing shares from a founder or employee—everything can still make economic sense, but QSBS may not follow the shares the way people intuitively assume.

Angels also run into QSBS complexity because angels love entities. Syndicates. SPVs. LLCs. Family investment vehicles. Advisory arrangements. Those structures can be smart and still require care if the goal is to preserve the exclusion at the investor level. The "who owns it" part of the QSBS story can be as decisive as the "what did we buy" part.

The angel's advantage is diligence. The angel's risk is assuming that diligence stops at the term sheet.

The punchline: QSBS is not a badge, it's a condition

People talk about QSBS as if it's a label that gets stamped on a stock certificate: *Qualified Small Business Stock.* As if you can put it in a drawer and take it out five years later, still qualified, like a bottle of wine.

In practice, QSBS behaves more like a condition with ongoing requirements. You don't just "have QSBS." You have stock that *may produce* an exclusion *if* the conditions are satisfied when you sell—and many of those conditions are about the past: how you acquired it, what the corporation did during your holding period, whether the corporation stayed within the asset and business-type rules, and whether there were transactions (including certain redemptions) that poison the qualification.

That's why QSBS is so emotionally brutal when it goes wrong: the sale happens, the gain is real, and then you learn the paperwork choices from years earlier quietly removed the benefit. The number on the tax return doesn't care that you didn't know.

So the practical way to think about QSBS is as *a fragile multiplier on your outcome*. The business outcome is hard enough. QSBS is the part you can protect with a small amount of early attention, and lose with a small amount of early carelessness.

"Protect it from day one" means treating equity like evidence

QSBS planning is less about cleverness and more about treating your equity as if someone might someday ask you to prove what happened.

Not a hostile someone. Just the normal someone: your CPA at exit, a buyer's diligence team, or the IRS if the numbers are large enough to invite questions.

The evidence that tends to matter is surprisingly unglamorous:

- *The exact date you acquired the stock.* Not the day you joined the company. Not the day the board "approved" something in a meeting. The acquisition date that controls your holding period.
- *How you acquired it.* Direct issuance from the corporation is a different creature than buying from another holder.
- *What you paid (or what was treated as paid).* That number feeds basis and can shape planning choices later.
- *What the company was at that time.* A company's size and activities when stock is issued can be the pivot point for qualification.

If you're allergic to admin work, it helps to reframe this. You're not "saving documents." You're storing the ingredients list for a future tax benefit. Without it, you're asking someone years later to reconstruct a recipe from memory—after the kitchen has burned down, the staff has changed, and the company has been acquired.

A plain-English view of the biggest misunderstanding: "I have startup stock, so I have QSBS"

Startup stock is common. QSBS is conditional.

Here are the misunderstandings that show up over and over, stated the way people actually say them:

- *"I bought shares from an early employee, so it's the same as investing early."* Economically, maybe. QSBS-wise, not necessarily.
- *"I've been at the company for five years, so my equity is QSBS."* Time employed isn't the holding period. What you actually own, and when you acquired it, is the holding period.
- *"The company is a tech company, so it should qualify."* "Tech" is a vibe, not a tax category. The actual business activities—and sometimes the way revenue is earned—matter.
- *"We'll fix anything weird right before the sale."* QSBS problems are often historical. Some can't be fixed retroactively at all.

The reason these misunderstandings persist is that they're reasonable. In startup life, we use broad words—equity, shares, ownership, vested, exercised—and we rely on social understanding. The tax law is not social. It is literal.

If you take nothing else from a plain-English treatment of Section 1202, take this: *QSBS is literal-minded. Treat it accordingly.*

Why the holding period feels longer than it is (and sometimes shorter)

QSBS has always rewarded patience, but the way people experience "time" with startup equity is strangely distorted.

Founders and employees often feel like they've been "in it" from the beginning, because emotionally they have. They remember the first office, the first prototype, the first customer. That sense of time is real—and it's also unrelated to the legal start of your QSBS holding period if you didn't actually acquire stock back then.

Investors experience the opposite distortion. Angels often know the exact day the wire went out. They can tell you the closing date. But they may not realize their ownership can later be reshaped by things that happen at the company level: restructurings, redemptions, or other transactions that make a previously clean story less clean.

Under the expanded 2025 rules for stock acquired after July 4, 2025, holding period milestones can matter even before the classic five-year mark, which makes "when did I actually acquire the stock?" even less forgiving. A few months'slippage can move you from one tier to another, or from a partial exclusion to none at all, depending on how the exit lines up.

The boring takeaway is the useful one: treat the acquisition date as a first-class fact. Put it somewhere you will still have access to when your inbox is different and your life is different.

QSBS doesn't just ask "what is the company?" It asks "what was the company *while you held the stock*?"

People love to think of companies as nouns. "We're a software company." "We're a fintech company." "We're an AI company." QSBS forces you to think of the company as a verb: what it *does*, day after day, year after year, while you own the shares.

That matters because many of the QSBS requirements aren't a one-time certification at the moment of issuance. They have a "substantially all" flavor—meaning the company needs to stay within the boundaries for most of the period you hold the stock. The details can get technical, but the plain-English concept is straightforward: if the benefit is meant to reward long-term investment in an operating business, the business has to actually operate like an operating business, not drift into something that looks more like passive investing or a disqualified services model.

This is where QSBS gets psychologically tricky for founders. Growth often comes with tempting "smart" moves: holding lots of idle cash, buying real estate, building a side investment portfolio, acquiring companies with very different profiles, or monetizing the brand in ways that change the nature of the revenue.

Some of those moves are totally normal. Some are even wise. But once you care about QSBS, you also care about how those moves look through the narrow window of Section 1202's rules.

The point isn't to run your company for taxes. It's to avoid accidentally running your QSBS off the road while you're focused on building the business.

Why "paperwork problems" are usually "people problems"

When QSBS fails, it's tempting to blame paperwork. Missing documents. Incorrect dates. Sloppy cap tables. But paperwork is usually just the visible symptom of something more human:

- Nobody owned the responsibility.
- Everybody assumed somebody else was tracking it.
- The company moved fast and treated legal hygiene as optional.
- A founder or executive made a well-intentioned exception ("we'll just do this one thing") that changed the facts.

QSBS has an almost unfair relationship with "exceptions." Startups run on exceptions. QSBS breaks on exceptions.

That doesn't mean you should become rigid. It means you should become intentional. When something unusual happens—an equity buyback, a last-minute transfer, a secondary sale, a change in entity ownership, a repurchase from a departing employee—that's when QSBS deserves a tiny pause and a real question: *does this change the three-part story (stock, company, shareholder) in a way that matters?*

If you build that reflex early, it's astonishing how little extra work QSBS requires. Most of the work is simply refusing to let "we'll clean it up later" become the default.

A founder-and-investor way to talk about QSBS without sounding like a tax person

There's a practical communication benefit to having a plain-English QSBS vocabulary: it helps you ask the right questions without turning every conversation into a seminar.

Here are phrases that tend to unlock useful answers:

- *"Is this stock issued by the company or coming from someone else?"*
- *"What date will my holding period start—grant, exercise, conversion, or issuance?"*
- *"Who will be the legal owner—me, a trust, an LLC, or an SPV?"*
- *"Are there any planned redemptions or buybacks around this issuance?"*
- *"Is the company staying within the kind of operating business QSBS expects?"*

Notice what's missing: citations, jargon, and bravado. Good QSBS planning conversations feel like risk management, not like flexing.

The core mindset: don't hunt for QSBS at exit time

The worst time to "get serious" about QSBS is when you're already negotiating a sale. At that point, you're trying to do two hard things at once: close a complex transaction *and* reverse-engineer years of equity history under time pressure. Buyers, bankers, and lawyers will be sprinting. Your documents will be scattered. People who knew the early facts may be long gone.

The better approach is almost boring in its simplicity: treat QSBS as a feature of your equity that you maintain the way you maintain code quality or security hygiene. Not perfectly, not obsessively, but deliberately and consistently.

That means:

- When you acquire equity, capture the facts that start the clock.
- When the company does something unusual with equity, pause long enough to ask whether it changes qualification.
- When ownership changes—gifts, trusts, entity contributions—treat it as a QSBS event, not just an estate-planning event.
- When the company evolves, recognize that "we're still a startup" is not the same as "we still fit the QSBS profile."

QSBS rewards the kind of person who plays offense early and plays defense quietly. If you do that, Section 1202 stops feeling like a mysterious tax perk and starts feeling like what it really is: a high-stakes incentive that Congress designed to be claimed by people who took real risk—and were disciplined enough to preserve the benefit while they did.

1.2 Why the Tax Savings Can Be So Large

Startup equity has a funny habit: it feels small when you get it and enormous when you sell it. That emotional whiplash is exactly where QSBS earns its reputation. The rule isn't powerful because it shaves a little off your tax rate. It's powerful because it can erase tax on the *gain*—the part that tends to explode when a company goes from "scrappy" to "acquired."

Everything starts with one plain formula:

$$\textit{Capital gain} = \textit{sale price} - \textit{tax basis}$$

Tax basis is your starting point for measuring profit. In human terms, it's what the tax system treats as your "money in." If you bought shares for $10,000, your basis is usually $10,000. If you paid $0.01 per share for founder common at formation, your basis might be a number so small it feels like a rounding error. Basis is boring—until it isn't.

Because the day you sell, the IRS doesn't care how meaningful your equity felt when you got it. The IRS cares about the math.

The part people underestimate: appreciation is the business model

Most financial assets grow like a staircase. Salary grows annually. Real estate often grinds upward. A diversified index fund moves in inches.

Startup equity grows like a trapdoor. For years it can look flat—illiquid, hard to price, emotionally "valuable" but economically hypothetical. Then a priced round happens. Or a term sheet lands. Or a strategic buyer decides your product is cheaper to buy than to build. Suddenly the value isn't a dream; it's a wire.

That's why the same person can be simultaneously thrilled and nauseous at exit. They see a big number and immediately realize: "Wait, I have to pay taxes on this."

Yes. Normally you do. And the taxes can be surprisingly large because the *gain* is surprisingly large.

A simple example shows the mechanics without needing any tax jargon:

- You acquire stock early for $20,000 total.
- Years later, you sell it for $2,020,000.
- Your capital gain is $2,000,000.

The gain is what gets taxed. Not the sale price. Not the headline. The gain.

Now take that same idea and dial it up to the way startup outcomes actually look when they work. Founders and early employees regularly have basis measured in hundreds or thousands of dollars. Angels can have basis in the tens or hundreds of thousands. The exit value can be seven, eight, nine figures.

This is the engine: tiny basis, huge appreciation.

QSBS is unusual because it attacks the largest number in the equation

Most tax planning in the startup world is incremental. You're optimizing rates, timing, or deductions. You're changing the *percentage* applied to the gain, not the existence of the gain itself.

QSBS is different. When it applies, it can exclude a meaningful share of the gain from federal taxation. That is not a "nice benefit." That is a different universe.

To appreciate why, it helps to separate two ideas people often blend together:

- A *rate* benefit reduces the percentage you pay on the gain.
- An *exclusion* benefit reduces the amount of gain that gets taxed at all.

A rate benefit is a discount. An exclusion can be an eraser.

And startup exits are one of the few times in normal life when an eraser matters more than a discount, because the taxable number can be so large that even "just" a few points is real money—and removing the tax base entirely can be transformational.

Basis: the tiny number that controls your biggest leverage

If you want to feel the power of QSBS in your bones, pay attention to basis.

Basis isn't just a line on a tax form. Basis is the control knob that interacts with one of QSBS's most important limitations: the *per-issuer cap*. The cap is structured as the greater of:

- a fixed dollar amount (commonly framed as $10 million per issuer per taxpayer under pre-OBBBA rules, and $15 million for QSBS acquired after July 4, 2025), or
- 10× your basis in the shares you sold.

That "greater of" structure is a big reason QSBS planning becomes a real discipline instead of trivia. It means the best possible QSBS outcome depends not only on your gain, but also on how you acquired your shares, what you paid, and what counts as basis.

It also means two people can sell the same company on the same day, at the same price per share, and have dramatically different maximum exclusions.

Here's the basic idea using nothing but round numbers.

How the 10× basis limitation can matter

Scenario	*Basis*	10× *Basis*	*Which Cap Likely Controls?*
Founder common at formation	$20,000	$200,000	Fixed dollar cap (e.g., $10M / $15M)
Angel seed check	$200,000	$2,000,000	Fixed dollar cap often still larger
Later-stage investor (still eligible)	$2,000,000	$20,000,000	10× basis can exceed fixed cap

A founder with very low basis often has a giant gain and a basis multiple that's small compared to the fixed dollar cap—so the dollar cap tends to be the binding limit. A later-stage eligible buyer (where eligibility exists) may have enough basis that the 10× basis cap becomes the bigger number.

That's why QSBS can reward both extremes: the person who got in absurdly early (tiny basis, huge gain) and the person who put in meaningful cash (big basis, potentially even bigger exclusion cap).

Why the fixed cap feels like a magic trick (and why it isn't)

When people first hear "exclude up to $10 million" (or $15 million for post—July 4, 2025 acquisitions), the mind does what it always does with big round numbers: it turns them into a promise. A guarantee. A perk you "unlock."

In practice, that cap behaves less like a prize and more like a ceiling. It doesn't create gain; it limits how much gain can be removed from taxation *if* the stock qualifies and *if* you have gain.

Two practical implications fall out of this:

- If your gain is $3 million, the cap doesn't matter—you're below it.
- If your gain is $60 million, the cap matters a lot, and planning starts to revolve around how many "buckets" you can legally create without breaking the rules.

The second point is where founders and angels start hearing about "stacking" strategies, gifting, trusts, and other techniques. Those can be legitimate, and they can also be booby-trapped. The important plain-English takeaway for now is simpler: *the fixed cap is the gate that turns QSBS from "nice" to "historic."*

And with the post-OBBBA fixed cap moving from $10 million to $15 million for eligible stock acquired after July 4, 2025, the gate got wider.

The real-world reason QSBS saves so much: concentrated risk creates concentrated gains

Most people don't build wealth the way startup equity builds it. Normal wealth-building is diversified and gradual. Startup wealth-building is concentrated and lumpy. You can work for years with no liquidity, then realize your biggest financial event happened in one signature.

That concentrated gain creates a concentrated tax bill.

Even if you never think about tax rates, you can understand the emotional impact: taxes become your largest "expense" on your best day. They can exceed your down payment, your student loans, your parents' mortgage, your first fund's entire committed capital—depending on the outcome.

QSBS matters because it is designed for concentrated, long-term, high-risk wins. If you're holding the kind of equity that might one day become the bulk of your net worth, you're exactly the kind of person who should care about a rule that can remove millions of gain from federal taxation.

Holding period: the calendar can be worth more than the negotiation

When people negotiate exits, they negotiate price, rollover equity, employment terms, escrow, reps and warranties—serious stuff. But QSBS adds a quieter dimension: the calendar.

Under the expanded 2025 rules for stock acquired after July 4, 2025, partial exclusions can apply at 3 and 4 years (50% after 3 years, 75% after 4 years, and 100% after 5 years). That changes the feel of timing. It means there are now multiple "cliffs" where an extra handful of months can change the portion of gain eligible for exclusion.

A plain-English way to see it is to imagine the same sale price but different closing dates:

- Sell at 2.5 years: potentially no QSBS exclusion from holding period alone.
- Sell at 3.1 years: potentially a 50% exclusion on eligible gain for post—July 4, 2025 QSBS.
- Sell at 5+ years: potentially a 100% exclusion on eligible gain.

That's not a moral lesson about patience. It's a financial reality about thresholds. For the right person in the right company, time can be worth seven figures.

This is also why sloppy recordkeeping around acquisition dates is so expensive. If the question is "did you hit three years?" the answer can hinge on the difference between an option grant date, an exercise date, or a conversion date. When your benefit changes at discrete milestones, "close enough" stops being close enough.

Cheap stock is the rocket fuel—until you remember taxes exist

Founders and early employees often talk about "getting in early" as if it's primarily about upside. It is. But it's also about something more mechanical: early equity tends to have very low basis, and low basis means almost everything you receive at exit is gain.

That's fantastic when you're looking at your net worth. It's less fantastic when you remember that gain is taxable.

This is where QSBS feels like it was written by someone who actually understands startups. It doesn't subsidize your salary. It doesn't reward you for taking money out. It rewards you for holding an illiquid, risky asset long enough that, if it pays off, the payoff is mostly appreciation.

So when someone says, "Why does QSBS matter so much to founders?" the answer isn't "because founders are special." The answer is: *because founder economics are gain-heavy.*

The "later-stage can still qualify" twist that expands the playing field

A subtle but important piece of the 2025 expansion is that the qualified small business gross-asset threshold increased to $75 million for QSBS acquired after July 4, 2025 (with inflation indexing after 2026). In plain terms, that can move QSBS from "only for the earliest days" toward "still possible later than you think," depending on the company's balance sheet at issuance.

That matters because many companies now look "too big" long before they actually feel big. A strong seed round, a hot Series A, or a capital-intensive model can swell a balance sheet early. Under a higher gross-asset ceiling, some businesses that would have aged out of QSBS eligibility sooner may remain eligible for longer—meaning more employees, more investors, and more rounds where QSBS planning stays relevant.

The practical effect is that QSBS planning is less niche than it used to be. More companies can plausibly fit inside the tent, which means more people will be tempted to assume they qualify, and more people will need to actually verify.

Why "QSBS only matters if you're rich" is backward

QSBS matters *because you might become rich on paper all at once.*

Many founders and early employees don't feel wealthy before an exit. They may be paying rent with a salary that's below market. They may have student loans. They may have kids. Their lifestyle can look ordinary even while they hold equity that could become extraordinary.

Then the liquidity event hits, and they have a high-income-year problem without ever having had high-income-year habits. They may not have estimated taxes set aside. They may not have a tax strategy. They may not even know what their basis is.

QSBS is most valuable to the people who wake up one day with a huge gain they didn't plan their cash life around. The exclusion can be the difference between "I sold my company and immediately owe a terrifying amount" and "I sold my company and have the liquidity to build the life I actually want."

A founder's mental model: QSBS is like an invisible co-investor who takes less

One way to make taxes feel intuitive is to imagine a silent partner who shows up at exit and takes a percentage of the gain. That's basically how capital gains tax feels. You did the work, you took the risk, and then a partner you didn't invite takes a share.

QSBS doesn't eliminate that partner in every case, but it can dramatically reduce their cut—sometimes to zero on eligible gain up to the cap.

That's why the "economic engine" behind QSBS is so compelling: it changes the split on the thing that matters most, the exit gain. Not the salary. Not the small perks. The big, lumpy payoff.

The practical habit that makes the math work: track basis like it's a receipt for your future

People track their startup equity like it's a story: "I joined early." "I have 0.4%." "I'm fully vested." Those are real facts, and they're not tax facts.

The tax facts you want to treat as sacred are:

- what you paid (or what was treated as paid) for the shares,
- when you acquired them, and
- what legal form of ownership holds them.

Basis is the receipt. If your basis is wrong, the gain calculation is wrong. If the gain calculation is wrong, the QSBS claim can be wrong.

And "wrong" is the kind of word that shows up at exactly the moment you can least afford it: after you've sold and spent.

People are often surprised by how messy basis can become in startup life—multiple exercises, different strike prices, partial early exercises, tender offers, conversions, and equity issued in different rounds. That messiness isn't fatal. It just means the person who keeps clean records quietly wins.

When QSBS is the difference between "good exit" and "great exit"

Imagine two founders who each sell stock for $12 million of gain that would otherwise be long-term capital gain. Same company. Same economics. Same effort. The difference is that one founder's shares qualify for QSBS and the other founder's don't, due to a fixable paperwork and timing mistake made years earlier.

Even without putting tax rates on paper, you can feel the gap. One founder keeps materially more of the most important check of their life. The other founder learns a painful lesson about how the legal system values precision over intention.

That is why QSBS inspires such intense reactions—almost evangelical enthusiasm from people who planned correctly, and genuine anger from people who discover late that they didn't.

The engine is not mysterious. It's simple arithmetic multiplied by startup outcomes:

Tiny basis + huge appreciation = huge gain.
QSBS exclusion applies to gain = huge savings.

And that's the reason the stakes feel so high. The benefit is tied to the part of the equation that scales without mercy when a startup succeeds.

1.3 The Readers, Scenarios, and Decision Points That Matter Most

QSBS rewards a particular kind of person: someone who took a real risk early, then kept their legal and tax posture clean while everything else got chaotic. That "person" might be a founder sleeping next to a laptop, an engineer with a half-forgotten option grant, or an angel who can recite a cap table better than a lullaby. Different lives, same trap: the best tax outcome often hinges on a moment that felt minor when it happened.

The useful way to think about QSBS isn't as a category ("I'm a founder, so I should qualify") but as a chain of decision points that appear at predictable times. Some of them are obvious (forming as a C corporation). Others are sneakier (a buyback to tidy up the cap table). The book is a field manual for those moments, but first it helps to know which moments tend to matter most for *you*.

Founders: you don't just own the risk—you create the facts

Founders typically have the highest ceiling for QSBS savings, and not because they're luckier. It's because founders tend to have (1) very low basis and (2) a lot of shares. That combination makes the gain at exit enormous, which makes any exclusion enormously valuable. Founders are also the people most likely to accidentally detonate QSBS for everyone else, because founders are the ones signing off on restructurings, redemptions, and "quick cleanups."

The founder-specific reality is that QSBS eligibility is often baked into the company's earliest habits. A startup can build a culture where equity paperwork is treated like production code—reviewed, versioned, and respected. Or it can build a culture where equity paperwork is treated like laundry—everyone means to do it, and somehow it never gets done until it's urgent.

The founder decision points that most often decide the QSBS outcome tend to cluster around six moments:

- *Formation and entity choice.* This is the "no do-overs" moment: the issuing company must be a domestic C corporation to issue QSBS. Conversions and reorganizations can be handled, but the cleanest QSBS stories start with the right structure.
- *Stock issuance hygiene.* Board approvals, purchase agreements, option plans, 83(b) elections when relevant, and clean cap table records. Founders can't outsource the responsibility for keeping these consistent—even if they outsource the paperwork.
- *Financing mechanics.* The QSBS story is usually strongest when investors are buying newly issued shares in primary financings. It can get murkier when the company encourages secondaries, does complex recapitalizations, or uses unusual equity instruments without thinking about downstream consequences.
- *Business model drift.* As we saw, what the company *does* can matter. Founders should be particularly alert when the business becomes services-heavy, reputation-driven, or begins to look like an excluded category. If the company's "real product" is the founders' expertise, the QSBS story gets stressed.
- *Asset and balance sheet management.* QSBS rules include an active business requirement that, in plain language, expects the company's assets to be used primarily in an active qualified trade or business during substantially all of the holding period. Founders influence this through treasury decisions, real estate purchases, and the temptation to park meaningful value in passive assets.
- *Redemptions and buybacks.* This is the silent killer. A repurchase can feel like a tidy, founder-friendly move—clean up a departing cofounder, help an early employee, resolve a dispute. But

certain redemptions around issuance windows can taint QSBS under Treas. reg. 1.1202-2. It's not that buybacks are forbidden; it's that the rules are specific and timing-sensitive enough that founders should treat "buy back some shares" as a legal-and-tax decision, not an admin task.

One founder scenario shows why this matters. Imagine a company that issues stock in an early financing, then decides to "simplify" by redeeming shares from a departing founder or other holders around the same timeframe. Nobody thinks of it as tax planning; it's just governance. But if that redemption pattern fits the wrong shape, later-issued shares that everyone assumed were QSBS may no longer be. That's a brutal outcome because the redemption felt like housekeeping, but it can change the story years later when the gain is real.

Founders don't need to memorize Treas. reg. 1.1202-2. They do need a reflex: *when a repurchase is on the table, QSBS is on the table too.*

Early employees: your risk isn't "wrong equity"—it's wrong timing

Employees tend to experience QSBS as a timing problem wearing a tax costume. Most employees don't negotiate entity choice or capital structure. They get an offer letter and an equity grant, and they focus on what any sane person focuses on: the job.

Then life happens. They leave. They get promoted. They move. They discover an old option grant in a dusty inbox. Or they receive an acquisition email and realize they haven't exercised anything.

The employee decision points that matter most usually revolve around the moment the holding period actually starts and who owns what:

- *Grant vs. exercise.* An option grant can feel like ownership, but the holding period that matters for QSBS typically starts when you acquire stock—often at exercise. Employees who wait may be shortening their QSBS runway without realizing it.

- *Departure windows.* Many option plans have short post-termination exercise windows. Leaving a company can accidentally force a major QSBS decision into a tight timeframe, when cash is uncertain and emotions are high.
- *Early exercise decisions.* Some plans allow early exercise. This can start the holding period sooner, but it's not automatically correct for everyone; it's a decision that blends cash, risk, and tax.
- *Secondary opportunities.* Tender offers and secondaries can be financially attractive, but selling early can collide with holding period thresholds—especially now that post—July 4, 2025 QSBS can offer partial exclusions at 3 and 4 years. "I can finally get some liquidity" is a powerful feeling; it deserves a calendar check.
- *Transfers and ownership form.* Employees sometimes transfer shares into trusts for estate planning or family reasons. Those transfers can be fine, but QSBS is literal: who owns the shares, and how the transfer was done, can affect the ability to claim the exclusion.

A particularly common employee scenario is the acquisition offer that arrives at an awkward age. The company gets a bid at roughly 3.2 years after issuance of post—July 4, 2025 QSBS. The board is excited. Employees are exhausted and thrilled. And suddenly the closing date becomes more than a corporate milestone; it becomes a personal tax threshold. Selling at 3.2 years can be meaningfully different from selling at 4.1 years, and different again from 5+ years, because the post-2025 framework offers 50% exclusion after 3 years, 75% after 4 years, and 100% after 5 years (for eligible stock acquired after July 4, 2025).

This can create a strange, very human tension: employees may want the deal to close because they want certainty, while the tax math quietly rewards patience. There's no universal answer. But the worst outcome is not "closing early." The worst outcome is *not realizing the calendar is part of the price.*

Angel investors: the most expensive mistake is buying the right company the wrong way

Angels tend to be the most QSBS-aware group in the ecosystem, and that's for a simple reason: angels often treat taxes as part of returns. They'll compare pro rata rights, liquidation preferences, and valuation, and then ask whether the investment is QSBS-eligible. That one question can make a "good" deal significantly better.

But angels also have a very specific vulnerability: secondaries.

A primary investment—putting money into the company in exchange for newly issued shares—usually matches the mental picture of what QSBS was designed to encourage. A secondary—buying shares from a founder, employee, or another investor—can make perfect economic sense and still be a QSBS problem, because the "original issuance" story can break depending on the facts.

Angels run into other recurring decision points as well:

- *How ownership is held.* Angels love SPVs and LLCs. Those can work, but pass-through rules can complicate who gets the QSBS benefit and under what conditions. The easy version of the risk: QSBS is generous, but it is not casual about ownership format.
- *Documentation at the time of investment.* Angels who invest across many companies may not realize that a future QSBS claim can hinge on seemingly dull documents: stock purchase agreements, capitalization tables, confirmations that the shares were issued by the company, and records of the company's size thresholds at the time.
- *Follow-on rounds and restructurings.* Angels often participate in multiple rounds. Different rounds can carry different QSBS

outcomes depending on timing, the company's asset threshold at issuance, and how the instruments convert.

- *Exit structure.* Whether an exit is structured as a stock sale or asset sale can matter, and angels should be allergic to assuming that "a sale is a sale." The QSBS benefit is tied to selling QSBS stock; a different transaction form can change the analysis.

The most common angel mistake isn't ignorance. It's optimism: "The company qualifies, so my shares should qualify." That's only true if the *way* you acquired them aligns with the QSBS rules.

A clean habit for angels is to treat "secondary" as a red-flag word that triggers a QSBS check—before wiring funds, not after.

Passthrough and trust owners: you can accidentally move the benefit away from yourself

Some of the smartest people in startup finance hold assets through partnerships, S corporations, LLCs, or trusts. Sometimes it's for estate planning. Sometimes it's for investing logistics. Sometimes it's for privacy, governance, or pooling capital. All valid reasons.

QSBS, however, can be finicky about who the taxpayer is and what kind of taxpayer they are. The benefit is generally aimed at non-corporate taxpayers. So if you hold startup stock through an entity, the planning question becomes: *who, exactly, will claim the exclusion when the stock is sold?*

With passthroughs, another question follows: *did the owner hold the interest at the right time, and do the pass-through rules line up with the holding period and eligibility requirements?* This is where "I own it" becomes an incomplete sentence. You want to know: *I own it how, and since when, and through what legal wrapper?*

Trusts add their own set of decision points. Transfers to trusts can preserve economics and still change the QSBS outcome depending on the type of trust and the timing of the transfer. Gifts and inheritance can preserve holding period in some contexts, but details matter, and QSBS is not a place to freestyle. If your plan involves moving shares to family members or to entities, you want that plan to be QSBS-aware from the start, not retrofitted at exit.

The key practical idea: *ownership form is not just an estate planning choice; it is a QSBS choice.*

The scenarios where QSBS is most often won or lost

Across all reader types, QSBS outcomes tend to pivot on the same handful of scenarios—not because people are careless, but because startups are busy and the consequences are delayed.

Scenario: "We'll do a quick buyback"

The company wants to repurchase shares from a departing founder or employee. It's sensible. It may even be necessary. But redemptions are specifically addressed under Treas. reg. 1.1202-2, and certain redemption activity around issuance windows can taint QSBS.

What makes this scenario so dangerous is that it often doesn't feel like "tax." It feels like HR, governance, or cap table hygiene. That's exactly why it needs a QSBS check: it's the kind of corporate decision that can quietly reach into every shareholder's future return.

Scenario: "Are we consulting? We're not consulting... right?"

Companies that combine software with implementation, advisory services, staffing, or highly relationship-driven work can end up in a gray zone. The tax law excludes certain service categories and also contains a "reputation or skill" concept that can make service-heavy models more uncertain.

A helpful anchor here is IRS PLR 202352009, which analyzed a staffing model and concluded it was not excluded consulting, illustrating how facts-and-circumstances can matter. The point isn't that every company should hunt for a PLR. The point is that businesses with services-forward revenue shouldn't assume they're safe just because they have an app and a website.

The earlier you assess how your revenue is actually generated, the more options you have if changes are needed. Once a company has five years of history, changing the narrative can be harder than changing the business.

Scenario: "I can finally sell some shares"

Liquidity is emotionally powerful. For founders and employees, a tender offer can feel like oxygen. For angels, a secondary can feel like good portfolio hygiene.

But QSBS is sensitive to timing. With the post—July 4, 2025 tiered exclusion structure for stock acquired after July 4, 2025, even the difference between 2.9 and 3.1 years can be meaningful. The decision isn't only "Do I want liquidity?" It's also "What does liquidity cost me in excluded gain?"

That doesn't mean you should never sell early. It means you should treat timing as a priced variable, not a footnote.

Scenario: "We're just putting this into an LLC / trust"

Transferring shares can be smart. It can also be the moment the QSBS benefit gets redirected, limited, or complicated—especially if the receiving entity changes who the taxpayer is or how the holding period and eligibility requirements apply.

This scenario is often a trap for sophisticated people. They know how to structure ownership for governance or estate planning, so they assume the tax benefit will follow automatically. QSBS doesn't reward sophistication; it rewards alignment. If you want the exclusion, the ownership structure has to be built to carry it.

Scenario: "We got big faster than expected"

Companies can cross thresholds quickly: a large financing, a big customer prepay, or an acquisition can swell gross assets or change the balance sheet. Under the post—July 4, 2025 changes, the qualified small business gross-asset threshold is higher ($75 million for QSBS acquired after that date, indexed after 2026), which can keep more companies in the game. But the threshold still exists, and the relevant moment is often the time of stock issuance.

This scenario matters for employees and investors who join later and assume, "It's still a startup." The QSBS question is narrower: "Did the company meet the size test when these shares were issued?"

A simple action list that catches most problems early

A good QSBS posture doesn't require a tax degree. It requires a few crisp facts that you can produce quickly when someone asks, years from now, "Why is this QSBS?"

If you only do one piece of homework, make it this:

- Identify *how* you acquired the shares you think are QSBS (new issuance from the company vs. secondary purchase vs. option exercise).
- Identify *who* legally owns them right now (you personally, a trust, an LLC, a partnership, an S corporation, an SPV).
- Identify *when* your holding period started for those shares (and keep the document that supports that date).
- Identify the future events most likely to change the QSBS story (redemptions/buybacks, transfers, secondaries, restructurings, or an exit that might close near a holding-period threshold).

This list works because it maps to the real failure modes. QSBS usually doesn't fail because someone misunderstood a footnote in the Code. It fails because someone didn't know which shares they owned, when they got them, what kind of transaction it was, or whether the company did something later that changed the conditions.

The people who win with QSBS aren't the ones who think about it constantly. They're the ones who know which moments deserve a pause—and they take that pause while the stakes are still small.

Chapter 2

The Foundations: Tax, Entity Choice, and Startup Equity Mechanics

QSBS can feel like a giant tax prize hidden behind small print. This chapter clears the fog. By the end, readers will understand the few moving parts that control most of the outcome: what your gain really is, when your clock actually starts, why your entity choice can make or break eligibility, and why not every piece of startup paper should be treated like stock.

2.1 Capital Gains, Basis, and the Math Behind the Exclusion

The happiest day in startup equity is usually a wire hitting your bank account. The second-happiest is telling your spouse you can finally stop refreshing the cap table like it's a stock chart. Somewhere between those two moments, there's a less glamorous question with real-dollar consequences: *what part of that cash is actually "gain" for tax purposes*? Not "how much did I make in my heart," but the number the IRS will treat as the thing that can be taxed—and, if you did the QSBS dance correctly, potentially excluded.

When people say "I sold for $12 million," they're usually describing *proceeds*: the money (and sometimes property) received in the sale. Proceeds feel concrete because they're what you can spend. But taxes don't care how exciting the number is; they care how much of it is gain. Gain is the spread between what you got and what you're treated as having invested in those shares over time—your basis after all the little tweaks, nudges, and paper cuts that happen across a startup's life.

That "over time" part is where most real-world QSBS stories get messy. Early equity starts simple. Then you exercise options. You do a tender offer. You pay a lawyer to clean up an ancient stock issuance. A merger turns stock into stock plus cash. You discover some shares were issued on a different date than you thought. You pay a broker. Someone with a spreadsheet rounds numbers. Years later, during acquisition due diligence, you learn your "basis" isn't just a line on a tax return; it's the narrative backbone of the whole exclusion claim.

Proceeds: not always the headline price

Proceeds sound like "sale price," but startup exits love fine print. Sometimes the press release announces a number that isn't what you personally receive. Sometimes you "sell" but keep rolling equity. Sometimes you get cash plus stock plus an earnout that may or may not ever pay. For tax math, proceeds are about what you receive for your shares, not what someone else's slide deck wants to brag about.

A few startup-flavored examples:

- *Cash at closing.* Straightforward: you sell shares for $X and receive $X (minus fees withheld).
- *Stock-for-stock merger.* You may receive shares of the acquirer instead of cash. That can still be proceeds, but the tax treatment can shift depending on deal structure. The key point for QSBS planning is practical: if you can't describe what you received with specificity (cash? shares? both?), you can't compute gain cleanly.

- *Cash plus escrow/holdback.* You might receive most of the cash now and some later, contingent on claims. Your proceeds may be recognized in pieces, and the paperwork will matter.
- *Secondary sale inside a tender offer.* You sell only some of your shares, not all. Proceeds are tied to the specific shares sold, which means basis allocation becomes the main event, not a footnote.

None of this is meant to scare you; it's meant to keep you from doing the most common founder math error: using the *deal headline number* as if it were your proceeds, and using "I paid basically nothing" as if it were your basis, and calling the rest a day.

Basis: the quiet number that drives everything

Basis is your tax "starting point" in the shares. You already know the concept; what's easy to forget is how many different paths lead to owning startup stock, each with its own basis mechanics. Two people can hold identical common shares and have wildly different basis because of *how* and *when* they got them.

Think of basis as your personal price tag attached to the shares. It often starts as what you paid, but it can also include other items the tax rules treat as part of what you put in. And later, basis can change—not because the market changed, but because the tax characterization of events changed.

Here are the most common startup ways basis gets set at the start:

Founders buying shares at formation

The "I paid $0.0001 per share" origin story is classic because it's often true. You form a corporation, you buy a large number of shares for a tiny amount of cash, and your basis is usually that cash amount (plus, in some cases, certain issuance-related costs that get capitalized). The good news is: this is the cleanest basis story on earth *if the paperwork is clean.*

The bad news is: founders are busy. They sign what counsel sends. They don't keep the signed purchase agreement. They change emails. They switch law firms. They assume the cap table software is the record. Then, years later, they're trying to prove they bought shares on a specific date, at a specific price, under an actual board approval. Basis becomes a scavenger hunt through old Google Drives and calendar invites.

Options: basis begins at exercise, not at the grant

Options feel like ownership because everyone talks about them like ownership. But for gain math, the basis story typically begins when you exercise and actually acquire shares. At that moment, your basis generally includes what you paid to exercise *and* (depending on the type of option and your personal tax situation) amounts that were treated as compensation income. This is one reason option exercises can produce tax forms and unpleasant surprises: the tax system may treat part of the value as wage-like income at exercise, and that amount can become part of your basis in the resulting shares.

Even if you don't want to memorize the rules, keep the mental model: *exercise creates a paper trail, and that paper trail drives basis.* If you exercised in multiple batches at different prices (or on different dates), you may have multiple "lots" of shares with different basis.

Restricted stock and vesting: what you paid, what was taxed, and when

Restricted stock can look like "I received shares, but they vest over time." The basis mechanics depend on what you paid (if anything) and whether the value was treated as income at grant or later as it vests. The point for QSBS math isn't to turn you into a walking regulation; it's to highlight a trap: two people can both say "I got

100,000 shares," and yet one has a crisp basis record and the other has a fog of vesting dates and missing valuations.

If your shares were subject to vesting, the documentation around the transfer, the purchase price (if any), and any elections or income inclusion can become the difference between a clean gain computation and a sleepless due diligence week.

Investors buying preferred stock in a priced round

Angel investors often have the cleanest basis story: they wire $X into the company and receive stock. Their basis is typically very close to the cash invested, and they usually have a subscription agreement, a wire confirmation, and a closing set of documents. If angels have problems, it's often because they invested through an entity (which can change who "owns" the shares for tax purposes), or because they later participated in secondaries and didn't track which shares were sold.

Adjusted basis: the number that shows up when life happens

The phrase "adjusted basis" sounds like accounting, but it's just a reminder that the basis you started with isn't always the basis you end with. Adjustments can increase or decrease basis depending on what happens to the shares and how those events are treated for tax purposes.

In venture-backed life, your share count changes constantly, but basis doesn't automatically "update" just because the cap table does. You can do a stock split, a reverse split, or a conversion and end up with a different number of shares without changing the total basis amount; it just gets spread across more (or fewer) shares.

A useful way to think about adjusted basis is: *basis follows your economic investment as the legal wrapper changes.* Sometimes the wrapper changes without you spending another dollar. Other times, you pay money (exercise price, broker fees) or recognize income (compensation components) and basis moves.

Common adjustment stories founders and early employees actually run into:

- *Stock split or reverse split.* Total basis stays the same, per-share basis changes.
- *Option exercises in tranches.* Each exercise can create a new lot with its own basis-per-share.
- *Broker and transaction fees.* These often reduce proceeds (or increase basis depending on how the fee is charged and reported). Either way, if you ignore fees, your gain number can be off.
- *Partial sales (secondary).* You must allocate basis to the shares sold. If you sell "some" shares, the basis story becomes lot-by-lot.
- *Corporate actions that change what you own.* Mergers, reorganizations, recapitalizations, or conversions can move basis around in ways that are mechanically logical but easy to lose track of if you only look at the final cap table.

The pattern is simple: exits force the math to become literal. If you can't support the adjusted basis number, you're not just risking a smaller exclusion; you're risking a larger taxable gain by default because the IRS doesn't give you credit for basis you can't substantiate.

Two startup scenarios where basis changes the ending

When people misunderstand basis, it's usually because they think it's too small to matter. In QSBS planning, basis has two jobs: it reduces gain (the obvious one) and it can also influence how much gain is eligible under the *10-times-basis limitation* (the one that sneaks up on people). A tiny basis can be great when a flat dollar cap is doing the heavy lifting. A higher basis can be valuable when you're trying to maximize the 10x-basis side of the equation.

Scenario A: founder common with a tiny basis and a huge outcome

You bought 5,000,000 founder shares for $500. Years later, you sell all of them for $20,000,000. Ignoring fees and complications, your gain is roughly $19,999,500.

That's the dream outcome. It's also the scenario where people get casual and say, "Basis doesn't matter." But basis matters in three ways:

1. *Recordkeeping.* If you can't prove the $500, the tax system doesn't automatically assume it. Missing basis generally doesn't help you.
2. *Share identification.* If you sold some shares earlier (a secondary), you might not be selling the same "lot" you think you are.
3. *The 10x-basis limitation.* Ten times $500 is $5,000. That limitation may or may not be your binding constraint depending on the rules applicable to you, but it's never fun to realize your basis is so tiny that the 10x calculation is basically irrelevant.

The practical takeaway: a tiny basis is not a problem; a tiny basis *with missing documentation* is.

Scenario B: employee exercises options, basis becomes meaningful, then sells part of the position

An early employee exercises 200,000 options at $1.00/share, paying $200,000. Assume their exercise also triggers some taxable compensation element that ends up reported and increases their basis further (the details vary; the point is that basis can be more than the exercise check).

A few years later there's a tender offer: they sell 80,000 shares for $25/share, receiving $2,000,000.

Now basis is no longer a rounding error. The employee must allocate basis to the 80,000 shares sold. If they exercised in multiple batches, they need to know which batch they sold (or what default method applies). If they can't identify lots and basis, their tax reporting becomes guesswork. Guesswork is expensive when the numbers have commas.

This is also where QSBS planning becomes personal instead of theoretical: if you're managing holding periods and exclusion strategies, lot-by-lot detail determines whether you're selling the shares that qualify when you want them to, and whether you can defend the gain computation that the exclusion will apply to.

The "basis file" you'll wish you had during diligence

Buyers, underwriters, and tax advisors don't want your vibes; they want your documents. The fastest way to turn an acquisition into a stressful audit-prep exercise is to realize your basis story lives in five different places: a cap table tool, a law firm's closing binder, a payroll provider, a brokerage portal, and an email thread titled "final_final2.pdf."

Treat your basis like a startup asset. Create a folder. Keep it boring. Keep it complete. The point is not to become a tax nerd; it's to avoid reconstructing your financial history from memory when the stakes are high.

Here's a practical checklist of what to keep, organized the way diligence tends to demand it:

- *Stock purchase agreements and subscription documents* for every stock acquisition (founder purchase, angel round, employee early exercise purchase, etc.), signed and dated.

- *Board consents and stock issuance approvals* tied to your issuance (especially early founder issuances and option exercises).
- *Proof of payment* (wire confirmations, canceled checks, brokerage confirmations) matching what you paid for the shares or to exercise.
- *Option grant notices, exercise agreements, and exercise confirmations*, including the number of shares, exercise price, exercise date, and any brokerage statements if a broker-assisted exercise was used.
- *Evidence of any tax amounts treated as compensation income* connected to equity (e.g., forms that show what was included in income). Even if you don't fully understand the tax mechanics, having the documents allows an advisor to compute basis correctly later.
- *Cap table reports at key dates* (formation, each financing close, each tender offer, each major reorganization). A current cap table is helpful; a historical cap table is a lifesaver.
- *Records of stock splits, reverse splits, and recapitalizations* (company notices, amended charter filings, and any cap table "before/after" summaries).
- *Documents for any gifts or transfers* of shares (gift letters, transfer agreements, updated stock ledgers). Even if the transfer is nontaxable at the time, it can become central later when establishing who owns the shares and what basis carries over.
- *Secondary sale documents* (tender offer materials, purchase agreements, trade confirmations) that clearly identify how many shares were sold, on what date, at what price, and what fees were netted.
- *A simple "equity ledger" spreadsheet* you maintain for yourself: date acquired, instrument type, number of shares, price paid, exercise price, and notes on any unusual features. It doesn't replace legal documents; it keeps you from getting lost in them.

The goal of this file isn't perfection. It's defensibility. If you can tell a clean story about what you own, when you acquired it, what you paid (in cash and in taxable income), and what you received when you sold, you've already solved the hardest part of QSBS math. Everything else is applying rules to numbers you can actually prove.

And that's the real twist: the exclusion feels like the star of the show, but the supporting actor that determines whether the ending is triumphant or tedious is the humble, stubborn, easily-misplaced basis record.

2.2 Holding Periods and Why Timing Language Matters

Tax law keeps time like a suspicious bouncer: it doesn't care how long you *meant* to stay, it cares what's stamped on your wrist. People talk about "a year," "three years," "five years" the way you talk about "around 7 p.m." at dinner. The IRS talks about time the way airports talk about liquids: exact, literal, and not impressed by your explanation.

That literalism matters because your gain can change character based on how long you held the asset. Form 8949's instructions boil the basic idea down to a bright line: a holding period of *1 year or less* is short-term, and *more than 1 year* is long-term. That phrasing—*more than*—is the tell. It's not "one year-ish." It's not "by the one-year anniversary." It's the day *after* you cross the line.

QSBS planning adds its own clocks, and the same unforgiving grammar shows up again: "more than three years," "more than five years," and (under the 2025 expansion) tiered outcomes that can make an extra year feel like an extra lever on your wealth. You don't need to memorize every threshold to get value from the concept: when the law uses "more than," it's inviting you to respect the calendar.

When the clock usually starts: ownership, not intention

A holding period begins when you acquire the asset—when you own the stock, not when you first heard about it, not when it appeared in a cap table tool, and not when you finally felt emotionally committed to the company. In common contexts, the IRS measures the start with maddening precision: the clock typically starts the *day after* acquisition (a tiny rule with big consequences when you're selling near a boundary).

That "day after" detail is why lawyers and tax advisors can sound overly pedantic about dates. They're not being precious; they're trying to avoid a one-day problem that can convert a favorable outcome into an expensive one with no change in the deal economics.

Here's a clean mental model that holds up surprisingly well in real life:

> *Your holding period is a story told in dates. If the dates are fuzzy, the story is weak.*

The story gets complicated because what feels like a single act—"I joined early and got equity"—often contains multiple legal events spread over months or years.

The anniversary trap: "one year" isn't one year

Most people instinctively think anniversaries are milestones. Tax law thinks anniversaries are *near* milestones.

If you bought shares on June 30, 2025, your one-year anniversary is June 30, 2026. But "more than one year" generally means you need to hold *past* the anniversary. Selling *on* the anniversary can still land on the wrong side of the line. The law's language is intentionally boring, and that's the danger: it looks like ordinary English, but it behaves like a switch.

This is why last-minute deal pushes are so emotionally taxing for founders. When the buyer wants to close on Tuesday instead of Wednesday, it can feel like a scheduling preference. If Tuesday is the day that makes your holding period "one year or less" (or "not more than three years," or "not more than five years"), Tuesday is not neutral.

And because the holding period often begins the day after acquisition, the "safe" closing day might be one day later than your gut expects.

What starts the QSBS clock: stock, not "equity-ish"

QSBS applies to stock, and the QSBS holding period is ultimately about how long you held that stock. That sounds obvious until you list the things people call "equity" that are not stock yet:

- an option grant
- an unconverted SAFE
- an unconverted convertible note
- a warrant that hasn't been exercised

Those instruments can be economically meaningful and emotionally motivating. They can even be tradable in certain contexts. But they usually don't start the stock holding period because you don't yet own stock. The clock tends to start when the instrument turns into actual shares.

A practical consequence: the date you *started working* and the date you *received an equity award* are often irrelevant to the holding period of the shares you later sell. That can be a painful realization for someone who's been "in it for years" but only exercised options recently.

Options: the grant is a promise; the exercise is the starting gun

Options are the most common source of timing confusion because the option grant feels like ownership. You were offered equity. You negotiated equity. You watch equity value rise and fall in your head. But the option itself is a right to buy shares later. The holding period for the shares generally begins when you exercise and actually acquire the stock.

That's not a technicality; it's the core feature of an option. Until you exercise, you're holding a contract, not the shares.

A scenario that shows how this bites:

- Year 1: You receive an option grant.
- Year 3: You finally exercise, perhaps because the company is doing well, or because you're leaving and need to exercise before a post-termination window expires.
- Year 4: A buyer shows up with a great offer.

From the outside, you've been associated with the company for four years. From the holding-period perspective for the shares, you may have held them only since Year 3. If the exit happens "too soon," you can miss a timing threshold even though you've been part of the ride for a long time.

Two practical lessons fall out of this:

1. *Exercise timing is holding-period timing.* Treat exercise decisions as calendar decisions, not just cash-flow decisions.
2. *Keep the exercise paperwork.* The exercise date is often the controlling date, and proving it later is not something you want to improvise.

Restricted stock: sometimes the clock starts earlier than you think

Restricted stock can be the mirror image of options. With restricted stock, you may acquire actual shares up front, but they are subject to vesting or forfeiture conditions. From a holding-period perspective, what matters is whether the stock is considered transferred to you and when you're treated as the owner for tax purposes.

That can produce outcomes that feel counterintuitive to people who think vesting equals ownership. In practice, a founder who purchases restricted stock at formation may have a holding period that begins very early (subject to the specifics of the arrangement), even though the shares vest over time. The documents, and any elections or tax treatment tied to them, can affect the timing story.

The stakes here aren't theoretical. A founder can have the most favorable holding-period profile in the room and still struggle to prove it if the formation documents are messy. Timing benefits are only as good as your ability to defend the dates.

SAFEs and convertible notes: your "investment date" may not be your stock date

Angels and early supporters often think of their holding period as starting when they wired money on a SAFE or a convertible note. Economically, that's reasonable: you put capital at risk on Day 1. Legally, you typically haven't acquired stock on Day 1. You've acquired a contract (SAFE) or debt (note) that may later convert into stock on a financing or other trigger.

In many common structures, the stock holding period begins when the instrument converts and shares are actually issued. That can shrink what you thought was a long hold into something shorter—especially in companies that stay in SAFE-land for years and then convert right before a fast exit.

This is also where "I've held this for five years" can be both true and false, depending on what "this" refers to. You held the instrument for five years; you may have held the *stock* for much less. QSBS is about the stock.

None of this means SAFEs and notes are bad. It means you should treat the conversion date as a date worth circling, saving, and documenting. If you can't point to when the instrument converted and how many shares were issued, you don't have a timing story yet—you have a hope.

Tacking: when time carries over, and when it doesn't

"Tacking" is the tax concept that prior holding time can sometimes carry over to a new asset or a new owner. It's continuity: the law treats the new holding as an extension of the old holding instead of a reset.

People often meet tacking as a surprise rule buried in technical memos. It's more useful to think about it as a question you can ask in plain English:

> *Did anything happen that should reset the clock, or did the law let the clock keep running?*

Tacking can come up in a few common startup-adjacent moves:

Gifts and family transfers

If you gift shares to a family member, you're changing the owner. The tax system often treats certain gifts as carryover events where the recipient steps into the donor's shoes for key attributes, which can include holding period. The intuitive reason: a gift is not a sale, and the law often tries to avoid pretending a sale happened when it didn't.

But don't treat this as automatic magic. Family transfers are exactly where sloppy documentation goes to die. If a future QSBS claim depends on tacking, you want a clean paper trail: transfer documents, updated stock ledgers, and a clear link back to the donor's acquisition date.

Corporate reorganizations and "same investment, new wrapper" events

Companies recapitalize. They convert preferred to common. They merge. They restructure the cap table so the economics stay similar but the legal form changes. Some of these events are designed to be tax-deferred reorganizations; others create taxable events. In tax-deferred contexts, tacking can preserve holding period because the law sees it as a continuation of the same investment.

From a founder's standpoint, the danger is assuming that every corporate action preserves your clock. Some actions effectively swap what you own for something else in a way that resets timing; others preserve it. The only safe posture is to treat major corporate actions as "timing events" worth checking with counsel and your tax advisor, not as purely administrative chores.

Equity rollovers in an acquisition

Sometimes an acquisition gives you a choice: take all cash, or roll some value into equity of the buyer. That rollover may be structured in a way that's tax-deferred for some portion, and the holding period attributes can follow complicated rules. The human temptation is to focus on valuation, upside, and the buyer's brand—and to ignore what the rollover does to your timeline.

The timeline matters because it affects when you can sell the buyer's stock without triggering a different tax profile. Even if QSBS is not directly involved in the buyer's shares, holding period is still the lever that separates long-term treatment from short-term.

The one-day problem: why "close enough" is not close enough

Timing mistakes in equity don't usually happen because someone can't count. They happen because deals move fast, calendars get edited, and people use conversational language for precise thresholds.

The one-day problem comes in a few flavors:

- *Selling on the anniversary.* You assumed the anniversary day was "more than" the period. It often isn't.
- *Starting the clock on the wrong event.* You used option grant date instead of exercise date; SAFE signing instead of conversion; "started working" instead of "stock issued."
- *Backdated-looking paperwork.* The company documents are signed later than the effective date, or vice versa, and no one can explain it cleanly. Even when the underlying event was legitimate, weird paperwork creates doubt.
- *Multiple lots with multiple clocks.* You exercised options in batches, or acquired shares in different rounds. Some shares clear a threshold; others don't. If you sell a blended chunk without identifying which shares were sold, you can accidentally sell the "young" shares first.

That last point is especially brutal because it looks like a math error but behaves like a legal error. When you have multiple lots, the question "which shares did you sell?" stops being philosophical. It becomes the controlling question for your holding period and the tax character of your gain.

Calendar thinking for people who hate calendars

You don't need to turn your equity into a Gantt chart. You do need to know which dates deserve obsessive accuracy. A useful way to prioritize:

1. *Stock issuance dates* (founder purchase, restricted stock issuance, conversion issuance).
2. *Exercise dates* for options and warrants.
3. *Conversion dates* for SAFEs and notes, tied to the financing close that triggered the conversion.
4. *Transfer dates* for gifts, divorces, and other ownership changes.
5. *Sale dates* for secondaries, tender offers, and the final exit.

If those dates are correct and supported, most holding-period questions become solvable. If those dates are fuzzy, you end up arguing from vibes in a context that only respects documents.

A few real-world timing moves that deserve a pause

Some timing choices are optional. Others are forced by life. Either way, it helps to recognize the moments when a calendar decision is hiding inside what looks like a career decision or a liquidity decision.

Leaving the company

Departures often trigger option exercise deadlines. When people leave, they're busy negotiating severance, starting a new role, or mentally detoxing. That's exactly when they make rushed exercise decisions that set the holding period for future shares.

If you're facing a post-termination exercise window, treat it like a major financial decision with two dimensions: the cash and tax cost to exercise, and the timeline you're starting for the shares. Sometimes the right answer is "don't exercise." Sometimes it's "exercise now." Sometimes it's "exercise a portion." The point is that the holding period impact belongs on the decision memo, not as an afterthought.

Tender offers and partial liquidity

A tender offer can feel like found money: sell a slice, keep the rest. Timing turns it into a strategy question. If you sell shares that haven't cleared a relevant threshold but you could have waited, you've traded calendar value for immediate cash.

That trade can still be smart. The mistake is making it unknowingly. If you're within striking distance of a threshold, it's worth asking whether waiting is feasible and what the incremental benefit could be. You may decide the liquidity is worth it; you just want it to be a conscious choice.

Gifting shares before a liquidity event

People gift shares for estate planning, family support, or charitable goals. Timing matters because gifts can interact with holding period and gain recognition in ways that can be favorable or surprising depending on the facts. The tax system can be generous to properly structured transfers and unforgiving to sloppy ones.

If you're considering a gift and there's even a whisper of a liquidity event in the next year or two, treat the transfer date and documentation as sacred. "We'll paper it later" is how you end up with an awkward conversation where everyone agrees a transfer happened, but no one can prove when.

Document acquisition dates like you document ownership percentages

Founders obsess over dilution math, and for good reason. But holding period is another axis of value, and it's easier to lose because it doesn't show up as a percentage. A 1% stake with the right holding period can be worth more *after tax* than a 1.2% stake without it, depending on how the sale lines up.

The practical habit is simple: every time you acquire stock—by purchase, by exercise, by conversion—save a "date packet" the same day. Put the signed documents and confirmations in a single folder with a filename that starts with the date in YYYY-MM-DD format. Add a one-line note: "Acquired 50,000 common via option exercise at $X on date Y." This is not overkill. This is future-you being grateful that present-you was slightly paranoid.

Time is the sneakiest variable in tax planning because it's invisible until it isn't. Once a deal is on the table, you can renegotiate price, escrow, retention, even closing mechanics. You cannot renegotiate the calendar. The calendar has already happened.

2.3 Why QSBS Starts With the Right Entity

QSBS is picky in a very specific way: it's not a reward for being scrappy, or innovative, or underfunded, or even successful. It's a reward for owning a particular kind of asset. The statute ties the benefit to *stock in a C corporation* and requires that the corporation be a C corporation during substantially all of the taxpayer's time owning the shares (26 U.S.C. §1202). That single phrase—*stock in a C corporation*—quietly disqualifies a huge amount of "equity" that people assume will qualify someday.

This is why entity choice has such an outsize effect on QSBS outcomes. You can do everything else right: hold for years, keep immaculate basis records, avoid redemption landmines, sell at the perfect moment. If the company wasn't a domestic C corporation when the shares were issued (and for most of the time you held them), the QSBS conversation often ends before it starts.

The hardest part is psychological. Early on, entity choice feels like paperwork. It's a one-hour conversation with a lawyer when you'd rather be naming the product and shipping a landing page. But the entity form is not just a label; it's the legal "container" that decides whether what you're receiving is the kind of stock Section 1202 even recognizes.

Domestic C corporation: the gate you can't charm your way around

"Domestic" is the easy part: generally, formed in the U.S. "C corporation" is the part that trips people, because it sounds like a vibe ("venture-backed! ") rather than a tax classification.

For federal income tax purposes, a C corporation is recognized as a separate taxpaying entity. It files its own return and pays its own tax. That separateness is exactly what makes C-corp stock a distinct asset that can carry special tax attributes like QSBS. IRS guidance on forming a corporation frames it plainly: the corporation is its own taxpayer. IRS Publication 542 provides the practical grounding: a corporation is a corporation; it has its own tax life.

An S corporation is not a different state-law creature; it's generally a corporation that made an election to be treated as a pass-through for federal tax. That nuance matters because founders routinely say "we're a corporation" when they mean "we filed in Delaware," but QSBS cares about the federal tax classification.

An LLC is usually the opposite of a C corporation for this purpose. Most LLCs are taxed as pass-through entities by default (partnership for multi-member LLCs, disregarded entity for single-member LLCs), with income and deductions generally flowing to members. LLC "units" can be economically similar to stock, and LLC operating agreements can mimic venture terms. But QSBS is built around *stock*, and generally around C-corp stock.

One uncomfortable truth: you don't get QSBS points for "planning to convert." The law doesn't give you credit for intention. It cares what you owned when you acquired it.

Why investors push the C-corp button so early

Venture capital didn't fall in love with Delaware C-corps because they enjoy paying franchise tax. They fell in love with them because the structure is standardized, predictable, and plays well with how funds operate. QSBS is one more reason that same structure keeps showing up.

When a company is a C corp, everyone's holding the same basic instrument—stock—and most of the downstream mechanics (option plans, preferred rounds, tender offers, M&A) have widely understood rails. That standardization turns out to be a tax feature as much as a legal feature: fewer weird edge cases means fewer ways to accidentally blow up eligibility.

LLCs can absolutely raise money, issue profits interests, and build great businesses. But if QSBS is a serious part of the plan for founders and angel investors, the C-corp choice is often less "optimization" and more "admission ticket."

A compact decision matrix (useful even if you ignore QSBS)

The chart below is intentionally blunt. Real life has nuance, and advisors will add footnotes. The point is to give you a founder-friendly way to see why C-corps are usually the default when QSBS is on the table, and why "we'll fix it later" can be expensive.

C corporation vs. LLC: the "we'll convert later" mirage

The most common origin story is not "we chose the wrong entity because we were careless." It's "we chose the entity that got us moving."

An LLC is fast. It can be inexpensive. It fits the mental model of "we just want to split the economics and get to work." For certain businesses, it's the right long-term form.

But if a company begins as an LLC taxed as a partnership and later incorporates, the tax and legal steps can create a bright line: the stock you hold after incorporation may have an acquisition date tied to the incorporation event, not to the day you first started hustling. And because QSBS turns on C-corp stock, the time you spent as an LLC member can be irrelevant for QSBS purposes.

Even when the conversion is executed cleanly, "later" creates two specific problems:

- *Lost time.* Your stock clock typically can't start until stock exists. Converting years in means you've donated years to the calendar with no QSBS benefit.
- *Messy inputs.* Conversions involve valuations, capital accounts, membership interests, and legal steps that can complicate basis and acquisition-date documentation. Those are exactly the two variables you want simple when you're trying to claim an exclusion.

A subtle version of this problem shows up when founders "paper" equity informally early on. Someone has a spreadsheet allocation of LLC percentages. Later, the company incorporates and issues stock. The economic understanding may be fair, but the tax attributes attach to what was actually issued and when. If you can't point to signed documents and issuance records, the story becomes hard to defend when it matters.

C corporation vs. S corporation: the election that can quietly ruin the plan

S corporations are magnets for misconceptions because they sit in the middle: "We're incorporated, so we're good... right?" Not necessarily.

Remember the framing from IRS guidance: S status is an *election*. A corporation can be formed under state law and still be a C corporation for federal purposes by default; it becomes an S corporation if it files and maintains the S election and meets all eligibility rules.

From a QSBS perspective, the key point is simple: QSBS wants C-corp stock. Stock of an S corporation generally doesn't satisfy that requirement. And the QSBS rules also care that the corporation is a C corporation during substantially all of your time owning the shares. So "we were an S corp for a while, then switched back" can be more than a paperwork hiccup; it can taint the timeline.

Why would anyone choose S status? Because pass-through taxation can be attractive for profitable businesses: income flows to shareholders, potentially avoiding the "double tax" dynamic of C-corp earnings. For certain companies, that's a feature, not a bug.

The twist is that most venture-style companies are not trying to distribute profits along the way. They're reinvesting. They're building. They're aiming for a liquidity event. In that world, the C-corp form is often the more natural fit, and it keeps the QSBS door open.

How entity form shapes everyday equity mechanics

Entity choice isn't just about taxes at exit; it's about what equity even means while you're building.

Option plans and employee equity

C corporations are the native habitat of stock option plans and standard venture equity grants. Employees understand them. Payroll systems understand them. Investors understand them. When a company is a pass-through, equity compensation often morphs into profits interests or other arrangements that can work, but are less standardized and can confuse candidates who expected "options like my last job."

Standardization matters because standardization produces reliable records: board approvals, grant notices, exercise agreements, and cap table entries that line up. Those records later become the evidence for acquisition dates and basis—the nuts and bolts that turn a tax benefit from a theory into a filed return position.

Investor expectations and closing friction

Even angel investors who love your product may flinch at an LLC if they've been burned before. Not because LLCs are bad, but because LLCs can create K-1s, complexity around allocations, and unpredictable tax consequences. Many investors want the simplicity of "I bought shares; I own stock." They also want future investors to feel the same way, because today's cap table becomes tomorrow's diligence file.

When you choose a C-corp structure early, you're not only choosing a tax classification; you're choosing a language that the capital markets already speak fluently.

Why "ease of unwinding mistakes" matters more than you think

Founders sometimes treat entity choice as reversible, like switching email providers. It's not.

A conversion might be straightforward legally and still be complicated for tax attributes. And even when the conversion is textbook, you can create second-order issues that don't show up until the company is worth real money:

- *Inconsistent acquisition dates* across founders if some interests were formalized earlier than others.
- *Basis confusion* if people contributed services, cash, IP, or other assets at different times.
- *Option plan timing* if equity awards were promised before the corporation existed.

- *Investor clean-up demands* that force rushed restructurings right when you're trying to close financing.

The cost of these mistakes is not just legal fees. The cost is lost flexibility. If you needed an extra six months or a year to hit a more favorable time threshold, you may not be able to "wait it out" if the clock started later than everyone assumed.

A practical decision frame: choose the entity that matches the endgame

The most useful way to think about entity choice is not "which is best?" but "which matches what we're actually building?"

If the plan is to create a venture-scale company with outside investment, broad-based employee equity, and an eventual sale or IPO-style outcome, the domestic C-corp form is often the least surprising path—and surprise is the enemy of tax planning.

If the plan is a cash-flowing business where owners want pass-through treatment and distributions along the way, a pass-through structure can be compelling. It's just a different story, with different tax levers, and often without QSBS as the headline benefit.

The mistake is mixing stories: building a venture-style cap table inside an LLC because it feels easy today, then hoping a later conversion will retroactively turn time into QSBS time. Tax law isn't sentimental. It won't award you extra years for effort.

What to ask your lawyer and tax advisor before you file anything

Entity choice is one of the few early decisions that's both high-impact and easy to sleepwalk into. A short, pointed conversation up front can prevent years of cleanup later. Useful questions include:

- Are we forming a *domestic* corporation, and will it be treated as a C corporation for federal tax purposes?

- Is there any plan (or temptation) to make an S election? If so, what would that do to a potential QSBS strategy?
- If we are currently an LLC, what exactly happens to founders' acquisition dates and basis when we incorporate?
- How will we document issuances so that years later we can prove who acquired what, and when?

Those questions sound procedural. They're not. They're the foundation for whether your future exit is a clean arithmetic exercise or a forensic reconstruction.

If QSBS is the prize, the domestic C-corp is often the arena. Everything else is a different sport—perfectly valid, sometimes even better for the right company, but not the game Section 1202 is designed to reward.

2.4 What Counts as Stock and What Only Looks Like Stock

If you've spent any time around founders, you've heard a sentence like: "I have equity." The word *equity* is wonderfully versatile—it can mean stock, options, a SAFE, a convertible note, a promise in an email, or a screenshot from Carta. For QSBS purposes, that versatility is the problem. Section 1202 is not an "equity" benefit. It's a *stock* benefit, and the law cares about the moment stock actually exists.

That moment is often less cinematic than people expect. It's not when you accepted the offer. It's not when you got the DocuSign link. It's not when your friend said "congrats" and you updated LinkedIn. It's when the corporation legally issues shares to you (typically with board authorization, documents, and an entry in the stock ledger). If you can't point to that moment, you may not have started anything QSBS-related at all.

This isn't pedantry; it's how the tax rules distinguish an asset from a future asset. It's also why cap table timing matters. Your cap table is a record of what the company believes it has issued. The IRS is not obligated to share your cap table's optimism. The IRS cares whether you actually acquired stock and whether it was issued in a way that satisfies the statute.

A quick gut-check: "Do I own shares right now?"

Before diving into instrument-by-instrument nuance, there's a practical question that clears a lot of fog:

> *If the company were acquired tomorrow, would I be asked to sign as a stockholder, or would I be asked to convert/exercise first?*

If you'd sign as a stockholder, you likely own stock. If you'd be asked to convert, exercise, or otherwise "turn something into shares," you likely don't own stock yet.

That distinction matters because the QSBS clock generally attaches to the stock itself. As we saw with calendar math, your timeline can be long emotionally and short legally.

Common stock and preferred stock: stock is stock, even if the rights aren't equal

When people hear "stock," they sometimes picture a single thing, like a share of Apple. In venture-backed companies, stock comes in flavors.

Common stock is typically what founders and employees hold. It's often cheap early, and it usually sits behind preferred stock in liquidation preference.

Preferred stock is what investors often buy in priced rounds. It can have liquidation preferences, anti-dilution provisions, and protective provisions that make it feel like a more sophisticated instrument.

But for QSBS analysis, the headline is refreshingly simple: both common and preferred are generally *stock*. The rights can vary dramatically; the fact of "stock ownership" is what matters.

So if you bought preferred stock in a financing and the corporation issued shares to you, you're typically in "stock-land." Your basis and timeline may be more straightforward than you think.

The confusion tends to arise not from the type of stock, but from the things that aren't stock yet.

Options: the psychological ownership trap

Options are the most common "looks like stock" instrument in the employee world. The company talks about your option count as if it's your stake. You track dilution as if you already own shares. You might even be shown a "fully diluted" cap table where your options are treated as if they're already stock.

Legally and tax-wise, an option is a right to buy stock later at a set price. Until you exercise, you don't own the shares. And as noted earlier, the shares acquired on exercise have their own basis and their own timeline. Grant date is not the same thing as stock acquisition date.

This becomes painfully real in two moments:

- *Leaving the company.* Your option can expire if you don't exercise within a post-termination window. People discover they don't "have equity" the way they thought; they have a contract with a fuse.
- *A liquidity event.* Tender offers and acquisitions often require a clean cap table. That can mean you must exercise before participating (or you might be cashed out under separate terms). Either way, the timing can move from "someday" to "by Friday."

A subtle cap-table mistake: treating an unexercised option as though it's QSBS-eligible because you've been at the company for years. The time you spent holding the option doesn't automatically turn into time holding stock.

Warrants: options with a different origin story

Warrants are cousins of options. They're also rights to buy stock, often issued to investors, lenders, or service providers in connection with a deal. Warrants can show up in venture debt, bridge rounds, or strategic partnerships.

From a QSBS perspective, warrants generally create the same core issue as options: a warrant is not stock. It becomes relevant when exercised and shares are issued. If a warrant is exercised years after issuance, the "stock timeline" generally begins at exercise, not at the warrant issuance date.

The practical risk is the same: someone looks at a warrant issued early, assumes "we're covered," and then discovers the stock itself was only acquired much later.

SAFEs: the instrument that sounds like equity but often isn't stock

SAFEs are popular because they make fundraising faster and cheaper. They're designed to defer valuation battles and push the "priced round" complexity into the future.

A SAFE often references conversion into equity. It may even use the word "equity" in casual conversation. But Section 1202 benefits apply to stock meeting statutory requirements; instruments that are not stock (or not yet stock) typically do not qualify until an actual stock issuance occurs.

In plain English: a SAFE is often an IOU for future shares, not shares today.

This creates two common misunderstandings:

- *"I invested two years ago, so my clock started then."* You may have invested two years ago, but the stock might have been issued only at conversion in the priced round. If the company converts the SAFE right before an exit, your stock timeline can be surprisingly short.
- *"My SAFE says I'll get shares, so I already have ownership."* A SAFE is a contractual right. Stock ownership is a corporate issuance. Those are different acts with different tax consequences.

In many cases, the conversion event is the moment to document obsessively: the closing date of the round, the conversion terms, the number of shares issued, and the stock certificate or electronic issuance record. That's often the first day you can credibly say you own stock.

Convertible notes: debt wearing an equity costume

Convertible notes are debt instruments that can convert into stock. They come with interest, maturity dates, and sometimes security or covenants. They also come with the same QSBS-relevant issue as SAFEs: until conversion and issuance of shares, you typically do not own stock.

Convertible notes create a few extra wrinkles that trip up otherwise sophisticated investors:

- *Accrued interest.* Interest can convert too, potentially affecting how many shares you receive and how basis is computed.
- *Repayment vs conversion.* If the note is repaid instead of converted, you never owned stock at all. You made a loan.
- *Conversion timing.* Notes can convert automatically at a financing or be forced at maturity. Timing can be driven by the company's needs, not your calendar.

None of this makes notes "bad." It just means you should treat "I hold a note" as a fundamentally different statement than "I own shares," even if the economic intent is to end up as an equity holder.

Restricted stock and the 83(b) fork in the road

Restricted stock is one of the few instruments where you can have actual shares early, even though the company retains a right to repurchase if you leave before vesting. This is where people who learned "options don't start the clock" can overcorrect and assume "vesting doesn't count."

Restricted stock can start the stock timeline earlier because shares can be issued up front, subject to restrictions. The tax system then asks: when should you be taxed on the value—now, or as vesting occurs?

That's where the 83(b) election enters. Treasury Regulation §1.83-2 provides the rules for an election to include in gross income in the year property is transferred, rather than waiting for restrictions to lapse. The election is fundamentally about *tax timing*: you choose to be taxed earlier on the value at transfer (often low for founders), rather than later as vesting happens (potentially higher).

QSBS isn't the only reason people care about 83(b), but the election can shape the way your equity story is documented and the way your ownership is treated across time. More importantly for this discussion, restricted stock is a reminder that "vested" and "issued" are not synonyms. Vesting is a contract schedule; issuance is a corporate act. The IRS cares about the corporate act.

If you have restricted stock, treat the grant packet as a permanent record. It's the source material for proving when shares were transferred, what you paid, and what restrictions existed. Future-you will not want to reconstruct that from a Slack message.

Cap table reality: names don't matter, events do

One of the most consistent QSBS mistakes is trusting the instrument *name* more than the instrument *mechanics*. Startups are creative. Documents get renamed. People say "note" when they mean "SAFE" and "SAFE" when they mean "side letter." Someone will call their restricted stock "options" because it vests monthly and they've heard the word options more often.

Tax law doesn't care what you called it. It cares what happened.

Here's the only framing that reliably cuts through the noise:

> *QSBS analysis starts when stock is issued. Everything else is a prequel.*

So instead of asking, "Do I have a SAFE or a note or options?" ask:

- Was stock actually issued? If yes, what class (common or preferred), how many shares, and on what date?
- What did I give in exchange—cash, services, cancellation of debt, exercise price?
- Is there documentation showing board approval and issuance?

Those questions are boring. They're also the questions that determine whether you have a QSBS asset or a future possibility.

When corporate "cleanup" becomes a tax problem: redemptions as a cautionary tale

Corporate actions after issuance can matter too. A company can do something that looks like ordinary housekeeping—buying back shares from a departing team member, simplifying the cap table before a financing, cleaning up early investors—and accidentally step on a QSBS landmine.

As we saw, redemptions can be a silent killer. Treasury Regulation §1.1202-2 provides an example of how redemptions and buybacks can affect whether stock is treated as QSBS. The important takeaway here isn't the exact thresholds; it's the category of risk: *cap table mechanics are not just corporate law mechanics*. They can rewrite the tax story.

This is another reason to be precise about what you hold. If you're holding actual stock, corporate actions like repurchases can affect the stock's status. If you're holding a SAFE, those repurchase rules may not touch you yet—but they could matter later once you convert and become a stockholder.

Instrument-by-instrument: what to track so you're not guessing later

The biggest favor you can do for yourself is to know the "key date" for each instrument type—the date that tends to start the serious analysis.

- *Common or preferred stock:* the issuance date (when shares are actually issued to you).
- *Options:* the exercise date (when you acquire shares), plus grant date as context.
- *Warrants:* the exercise date (when shares are issued).
- *SAFEs:* the conversion date and the stock issuance details at the priced round (or other trigger).
- *Convertible notes:* the conversion date (or repayment date if it never converts), plus how interest is handled.
- *Restricted stock:* the transfer/issuance date, the vesting schedule, and any 83(b)-related documentation if applicable.

You don't need to be your own tax counsel. You do need to be able to answer, quickly and confidently, "When did I acquire the shares, and what documents prove it?"

The rule of thumb that saves people from bad confidence

People get into trouble with QSBS not because they're reckless, but because they're confidently wrong. They confuse proximity to stock with stock itself. They confuse "I have equity" with "I own shares." They confuse a contract right with a corporate issuance.

A clean rule of thumb keeps you honest:

> *If you can't point to the event where your instrument turned into stock and how many shares were issued, you're not ready to make a QSBS claim.*

That's not gatekeeping. It's self-defense. QSBS is powerful enough that it attracts scrutiny, and the strongest QSBS stories are boringly well-documented. The less your equity story depends on interpretation, the more it can depend on paper. And paper, unlike memory, doesn't get hazy when the exit finally arrives.

Chapter 3

The Core Eligibility Rules Every QSBS Claim Depends On

QSBS can feel like a golden ticket, but only if every link in the chain holds up: the right taxpayer, the right stock, the right company, and the right fact pattern over time. This chapter helps readers pressure-test those links early, so they can spot hidden disqualifiers before a financing, buyback, transfer, or exit turns a tax windfall into a missed opportunity.

3.1 Who Can Claim the Exclusion

QSBS is less like a coupon you clip and more like a tax attribute that *sticks to a taxpayer*. That sounds abstract until you watch a real exit unfold: stock gets sold, money moves, a K-1 shows up, someone files the return, and the IRS only cares about one question—*whose gain is it?* The name on the cap table is often a clue, not the verdict.

Start with the bright line that surprises first-time founders: Section 1202 is designed for *non-corporate* taxpayers. Individuals can use it. Many trusts and estates can use it. Partnerships and S corporations can act as "pipes" that pass the benefit through to their owners. C corporations, as a general rule, are where QSBS benefits go to die. If a C corp sells QSBS, the C corp is the taxpayer, and Section 1202 generally isn't available to it—so the exclusion doesn't magically reappear when that C corp later dividends the cash out to you.

That's the headline. The real work is learning to spot the taxpayer in the wild.

The taxpayer is the one who recognizes the gain (not the one who gets the wire)

People talk about "who owns the shares," but tax law is obsessed with something slightly different: *who recognizes the gain*. Those are often the same person. Sometimes they're not—especially once you add entities, family planning, and "helpful" structures suggested by well-meaning advisors.

A quick reality check: the wire can go to your household account, your holding company, your trust's bank account, or into escrow to pay off a loan. None of that determines who claims Section 1202. The claimant is the taxpayer who reports the sale on their return (or whose Schedule K-1 reports it to them).

If you keep one mental habit from this: before you reorganize anything, picture the future exit and ask, *Which taxpayer will show the gain on the tax return?* Then ask the second question: *Is that taxpayer eligible to claim QSBS?*

Individuals: the "default" QSBS claimant (and why simplicity is underrated)

For founders, early employees, and angels, individual ownership is the cleanest path. The individual is the taxpayer, the gain is the individual's gain, and the Section 1202 computation lives on that individual return.

Two details tend to surprise people even here:

- *Married couples don't create a new taxpayer just because they share finances.* Depending on how title is held and state property law, you might have one owner, two owners, or one owner for legal purposes but two taxpayers for economic purposes. The tax reporting follows the law of ownership and allocation rules—not your Venmo history.

- *Joint ownership is a planning lever, but it isn't a "free doubling" button by default.* Many couples assume "we'll just split the stock and get two caps." Sometimes that works with careful implementation; sometimes the timing, the transfer method, or the actual legal ownership makes the split less effective than the spreadsheet suggests.

The reason simplicity is underrated is that QSBS is *fussy about provenance.* If your fact pattern is clean—stock acquired and held by an individual, sold by that same individual—there are fewer places for a diligence reviewer to stick a pin and say, "show me the documents."

Two people, one household, multiple ways the IRS can view ownership

Married founders often treat equity as "ours," but the tax system has several competing lenses:

- *Title lens:* whose name is on the stock certificate or capitalization table.
- *Property-law lens:* in community property states, ownership can be shared by operation of law even if title is in one spouse's name.
- *Taxpayer lens:* who reports the income, which can follow property law, entity allocations, and return filing positions.

This becomes practical when someone tries to do a late-stage "QSBS fix" by moving shares around the family shortly before signing an LOI. Even if a transfer is legally valid, the IRS will look at whether the taxpayer claiming the exclusion truly owned the shares in the way Section 1202 contemplates, and whether the transfer fits within the rules that preserve QSBS character.

A cleaner approach is boring but powerful: if you anticipate family-level allocations (for example, between spouses), treat it like cap table hygiene—get the ownership aligned early, keep the paperwork tight, and don't wait until an exit turns the stock into a tax return line item with seven figures attached.

Trusts: a legitimate QSBS claimant, but only if you respect what a trust *is*

Trusts sit in the uncanny valley of tax planning: everyone has heard they're useful, many people use them, and plenty of people can't clearly explain who the taxpayer is once a trust enters the story.

At a high level, a trust can be an eligible QSBS claimant because it is not a corporation. But "trust" is not one tax creature. The big divide is whether the trust is treated as:

- *Owned by an individual for income tax purposes* (commonly called a grantor trust), in which case the individual is often the one who reports the trust's income, or
- *Its own taxpayer* (a non-grantor trust), in which case the trust itself reports the income unless it distributes income in a way that pushes it out to beneficiaries.

Why does that matter for QSBS? Because the exclusion attaches to the taxpayer reporting the gain. If the trust sells the stock, you want to know whether the trust is the taxpayer claiming Section 1202 or whether the grantor (or beneficiaries) are the taxpayers claiming it. That determines whose per-issuer cap is in play, whose return gets audited, and whether the person who can actually use the exclusion is the one holding the attribute.

Trust planning also has a human hazard: people hear "put the stock in a trust" and think they've done estate planning and tax planning in one move. Sometimes they have. Sometimes they've just changed *who* is allowed to claim QSBS without realizing it—and the new claimant might have less flexibility, different tax brackets, or different state tax exposure.

Estates: the forgotten QSBS claimant in founder planning

An estate can also be an eligible claimant. That matters in two ways.

First, it's a practical detail for the real world: founders die. Early investors die. If QSBS stock is still held at death and later sold by an estate, the estate may be the taxpayer recognizing the gain and therefore the one evaluating the QSBS exclusion.

Second, estate administration is document-heavy, and QSBS is document-hungry. If QSBS is going to be claimed by an estate, the executor will need what founders often misplace: issuance documents, subscription agreements, proof of when and how the shares were acquired, and enough corporate history to support the claim. The QSBS "file" you keep while you're alive becomes a financial asset for the people who clean up your affairs.

If that sounds grim, translate it into a founder-friendly incentive: keeping QSBS documentation tight is not just an exit move. It's basic asset stewardship.

Partnerships and LLCs taxed as partnerships: QSBS can pass through, but timing is everything

A partnership (including most multi-member LLCs) is usually a pass-through entity: it doesn't pay entity-level income tax like a C corporation; instead, it allocates income, gain, loss, and deduction to partners who report those items on their own returns.

That structure can work beautifully for QSBS, but it adds a time dimension that individuals don't face: the owners who benefit are generally the ones who were partners during the relevant periods and are allocated the sale gain under the partnership agreement and tax rules.

Here's the intuitive risk: a partnership buys QSBS, later admits a new partner, then sells the QSBS. The new partner may economically share in the profit (depending on the deal), but for QSBS purposes, you can't assume they automatically share the exclusion. Section 1202's pass-through mechanics can be unforgiving about who owned what, and when.

Two founder-adjacent scenarios bring this to life:

- *Angel syndicates and SPVs.* A special purpose vehicle (SPV) formed as an LLC taxed as a partnership can hold startup stock. QSBS benefits may flow to members. But the SPV's operating agreement, admission dates, capital account mechanics, and allocations start to matter—because they determine who recognizes gain and whether the QSBS story is coherent.
- *Family investment LLCs.* Families sometimes use LLCs to centralize investing. That can be sensible governance. But if family members are added later, or ownership shifts, you have to track whether the people expecting QSBS are the ones who can actually claim it.

A practical rule of thumb: partnerships can transmit QSBS benefits, but partnerships also create more ways to accidentally misalign legal ownership, economic deal terms, and tax reporting. If you like clean QSBS outcomes, you should like clean partnership paperwork.

S corporations: another pass-through "pipe," with its own quirks

S corporations can also pass items through to shareholders. Like partnerships, S corps are generally not the ones paying the tax on gain (with exceptions and complications outside our scope); shareholders are.

That means QSBS held by an S corporation can potentially yield Section 1202 benefits at the shareholder level—again, assuming the statutory requirements are satisfied and the right shareholders are in place.

S corps have their own brand of rigidity: one class of stock (in general), limits on who can be a shareholder, and strict compliance rules. The QSBS relevance is that S corps tend to be used by closely held groups that also love "cleanup" transactions—moving shares among family members, adding shareholders, shifting ownership before an exit. Those are exactly the moments where QSBS benefits can be accidentally stranded in the wrong taxpayer.

The headline caution is similar to partnerships but with an S corp flavor: don't assume you can reshuffle ownership right before a liquidity event and have the exclusion follow your intentions. In pass-through land, intentions don't file tax returns—taxpayers do.

C corporations: the QSBS dead end that still tempts people

Founders sometimes create a personal holding company or "blocker" C corporation for non-tax reasons: to pool investments, to keep a clean line between personal assets and risk, or because "that's what sophisticated people do."

With QSBS, that instinct can be expensive.

If a C corporation owns the stock and sells it, the gain sits inside the corporation. Section 1202 generally doesn't help a corporate taxpayer. Then, if you want the cash personally, you often need dividends or a liquidation—each with its own tax consequences. The math can turn an exit that could have been lightly taxed into one that gets taxed twice.

There are situations where a corporate holder still makes sense for other reasons. But QSBS is one of the strongest arguments for founders and angels to resist reflexively "corporatizing" their personal investment activity. If you're trying to preserve a tax exclusion meant for humans, don't interpose an entity that the statute mostly treats as ineligible.

"Owner on paper" traps: nominees, custodians, and the cap table mirage

The cap table is not scripture. It's a ledger. Ledgers can be wrong, incomplete, or misleading—especially after years of option exercises, early tender offers, platform migrations, and law firm changes.

A few patterns show up often:

- *Shares held through a custodian or brokerage name.* The record owner might be a nominee (like a brokerage) while you remain the beneficial owner. Tax reporting often follows beneficial ownership, but you want documentation that makes the chain clear.
- *Shares "parked" with a friend or early employee.* Sometimes a founder temporarily puts shares in someone else's name for convenience, credit issues, immigration reasons, or handshake deals. On exit day, handshakes don't determine who bears the gain; legal ownership and tax rules do. These arrangements can also create gift issues, compensation issues, and painful QSBS uncertainty.
- *Entity names that don't match reality.* People rename LLCs, merge them, or dissolve them without cleaning up the stock records. Later, they're stunned that the stock is still titled to an entity that no longer exists (or exists in a different form for tax purposes).

QSBS rewards clean chains of title. If you want the exclusion to be boringly reliable, treat ownership records as part of the asset itself. A messy cap table isn't just an administrative problem; it's a tax risk.

Transfers: gifting and family vehicles are not "just estate planning"

When people talk about QSBS "stacking," they often jump straight to the tactic—gifts to family members, trusts, or multiple taxpayers.

The deeper truth is that every transfer is a decision about *where the tax attribute will live.*

Some transfers can preserve QSBS character and allow the recipient to step into the seller's shoes for certain purposes; others can restart clocks, change eligibility, or create a claimant who can't use the exclusion effectively. The transfer can also create a new taxpayer whose return and state residency aren't what you assumed.

Even when a transfer is allowed, you're still left with the most practical question: will the recipient be the one reporting the gain? If the shares are transferred to a trust that later distributes proceeds, or to an entity that later reallocates economics, you can end up with a beautiful plan that works on a whiteboard and underdelivers on a tax return.

The cleanest mental model is to treat transfers as moving a valuable "QSBS packet" from one pocket to another. Before you move it, look at the new pocket and ask:

- Is this pocket an eligible non-corporate taxpayer?
- Will this pocket actually recognize the gain on sale?
- Does this pocket have any quirks—state tax, trust taxation, entity allocations—that make the exclusion less valuable than it looks?

Pass-through timing: the subtle reason last-minute restructuring disappoints

Founders love control. Taxes love timelines.

With pass-through entities, the ability to claim QSBS often depends on whether the owner was an owner of the pass-through at the right time—often when the entity acquired the QSBS, and certainly when the gain is allocated. That makes "I'll just add my spouse as a member" or "we'll drop this into an LLC" a lot less casual than it sounds.

The trap isn't that restructuring never works. The trap is thinking QSBS behaves like a sticker you can slap onto whoever you want right before the exit. In reality, Section 1202 has a memory. It remembers acquisition pathways and ownership chains. Pass-through entities add additional memory: who owned the vehicle, when, and on what terms.

So if you're thinking about changing ownership, do it with enough runway that the ownership story looks natural and well-documented—not like a frantic tax scramble triggered by a term sheet.

A founder-friendly way to identify the "real" QSBS claimant

If you're staring at a cap table and trying to predict who gets the exclusion, don't start with tax forms. Start with a simple narrative:

1. *Who will sign the sale documents?* (Individuals? Trustees? An entity manager?)
2. *Who will receive the Form 1099 or the K-1?* (That's a strong clue about who reports the transaction.)
3. *On whose tax return will the gain land?* (That is the claimant, or the entity that needs to push it through.)

Then match that claimant to a reality check:

- If it's a *C corporation*, expect no Section 1202 benefit (and plan accordingly).
- If it's an *individual*, you're in the cleanest lane.
- If it's a *trust or estate*, confirm who the income taxpayer is (trust/estate vs grantor/beneficiaries) and whether the structure aligns with who you intend to benefit.
- If it's a *partnership or S corporation*, confirm that the owners who expect the benefit are the ones who will be allocated the

gain, and that their ownership timeline lines up with the pass-through rules.

This isn't legal advice; it's a way to keep yourself from making the most common strategic mistake: spending time optimizing a QSBS outcome for the wrong taxpayer.

The practical takeaway: identify the taxpayer *before* you touch the shares

QSBS planning can be brilliant, but brilliance applied to the wrong owner is just expensive theater. Before any gifting, any trust funding, any SPV admission, any entity conversion, any "we'll clean it up later" cap table edit, lock in three facts in writing:

- *Who is the taxpayer today for these shares?*
- *Who is intended to recognize the gain on the eventual sale?*
- *Is that intended taxpayer an eligible non-corporate claimant—and structurally positioned to actually use the exclusion?*

Get those answers early, and a QSBS claim has a chance to be simple: the kind of simple where the exit is exciting for the right reasons, and the tax return is just paperwork—not a negotiation with your past self.

3.2 Original Issuance: How You Acquired the Shares Matters

Two shareholders can own the same class of stock in the same company, sell on the same day at the same price, and end up with totally different QSBS outcomes—because one of them got their shares from the company, and the other got them from another human. Economically, both "invested." Legally, only one may have stock that counts.

That's the original issuance rule in action. It's not a vibe. It's a provenance test: where did *your* shares come from?

The statutory instinct behind the rule is easy to respect even if you don't love it. Congress wanted to reward capital formation—money and sweat going *into* a small business—more than trading among existing owners. So Section 1202 generally wants the stock to be acquired at its original issuance from the corporation (directly or through an underwriter), in exchange for money, property, or services. The moment that chain breaks—especially via a secondary purchase—the QSBS story can break with it.

Think like a customs agent: "Where did these shares come from?"

If you've ever watched a big exit, you've seen this movie: bankers say "clean cap table," lawyers say "clean cap table," and someone eventually asks for the *chain of title*. That chain is the stock's passport. Original issuance is the stamp that lets Section 1202 through the border.

A useful way to frame it is to separate two categories:

- *Company-issued stock.* New shares created by the corporation and issued to you in exchange for money, property, or services. This is the lane Section 1202 is built for.
- *Shareholder-to-shareholder transfers.* You buy stock from another shareholder, or someone "assigns" you their shares. That may be a perfectly valid investment transaction—but it is usually not original issuance in the buyer's hands.

That sounds simple until you remember how startups actually operate. Equity doesn't arrive as a single clean purchase. It arrives as a sequence of documents: formation paperwork, restricted stock purchase agreements, option grants, exercises, SAFEs, notes, conversions, and the occasional "quick sale of some shares to cover a tax bill" that everyone promises is routine.

QSBS lives or dies in the sequence.

Founder stock: services count, but paperwork makes or breaks the story

Founders often earn their first shares with sweat, not cash. That can still fit the original-issuance requirement because original issuance can include stock acquired for services.

The trap is not that "services don't count." The trap is that founder equity is where casual behavior is most tolerated—and casual behavior is what QSBS later punishes. If stock is meant to be issued for services, you want a clean, dated issuance: board approvals (or incorporator actions), a stock purchase agreement (often a restricted stock purchase agreement), and proof the shares were actually issued on the corporate records.

Founders sometimes discover, years later, that what they thought was founder stock was actually a promise to issue founder stock. Or it was "issued" in a Google Doc cap table but never properly authorized. That's not just governance sloppiness. It can blur the "issuance moment" that Section 1202 cares about.

If you're the company, treat founder issuances like they'll be reviewed by a skeptical stranger in an M&A diligence room—because they will be. If you're the holder, keep copies like you're keeping title to real estate—because in a tax sense, you are.

The employee equity trap: option grants are not stock (and exercise mechanics decide the key date)

A common misread goes like this: "I got my option grant in 2019, so I'm already 'in the clear' by the time we sell." Options feel like ownership, and culturally they're treated like ownership. But for QSBS, the stock is the thing, not the promise.

For many employees, the real stock acquisition event happens at exercise—because that's when the corporation actually issues shares to you. That's also why the acquisition method is such an intense diligence item: cap tables frequently include mixed tranches with different origin stories (founder issuances, option exercises, secondary purchases, repurchases/reissuances). Your QSBS posture can turn on whether your shares were issued on exercise, whether the paperwork matches the intended exercise date, and whether the company had its own eligibility ducks in a row at that moment.

Even seemingly small exercise details can matter:

- *Exercise vs. "I clicked a button."* Many platforms make exercise feel instant. But the legal exercise date is the date the company actually receives a valid exercise notice (and payment, if required) and issues the shares. If you're relying on QSBS, you want those timestamps to be boringly defensible.
- *Net exercise and cashless exercise.* These are mechanically common, but they can complicate what you actually acquired, what consideration you paid, and what's documented. Complexity isn't disqualifying by itself; undocumented complexity is.
- *Same-day sale exercises.* In late-stage scenarios, employees sometimes exercise and immediately sell in a tender or acquisition. That may make sense financially, but it usually destroys the time needed for Section 1202 anyway. More importantly for this discussion: it highlights that the option itself is not the QSBS asset; the issued stock is.

The habit to develop is to treat the option exercise as a mini-financing: a real issuance event that deserves a file folder.

Restricted stock and early exercises: original issuance can be clean, but the timeline gets sharper

Restricted stock is often a founder's or employee's best friend for QSBS because it can put actual stock in your hands earlier—starting the clock earlier—if everything else lines up. Similarly, early exercise of options can move the stock issuance event forward.

But both create a sharper timeline: if QSBS hinges on original issuance, you must be able to prove when the stock was issued, under what authority, and what you gave in exchange. If your "early exercise" is missing evidence of payment, or if the company didn't properly issue the shares at the time, you can end up with the worst of both worlds: you thought you started early, but you can't support the date later.

Also, restricted stock introduces a second axis of confusion: vesting. Vesting affects forfeiture and compensation tax rules; it doesn't rewrite the fact of original issuance. People conflate these constantly because they experience vesting as "becoming real." For QSBS, reality tends to be more administrative: the corporation issued the shares, or it didn't.

Buying shares from a departing coworker: the classic secondary purchase faceplant

Here's the most emotionally frustrating QSBS failure mode because it feels so unfair. An investor buys stock from the company—potential QSBS. Another investor buys stock from an employee who's leaving—often not QSBS for the buyer, even if the employee's shares were QSBS in the employee's hands.

The economics can be identical. The check is the same size. The company benefits indirectly because an employee gets liquidity and stays happy (or at least leaves quietly). But Section 1202 generally isn't awarding points for "indirectly." It's looking for original issuance from the corporation.

Secondary purchases show up in more places than people admit:

- *Founder "rebalancing" deals.* One founder buys shares from another founder to "even things out."

- *Employee liquidity.* A new investor or existing investor buys shares directly from employees.
- *Angel-to-angel sales.* Early investors sell to later investors because they want to de-risk.

None of those are inherently bad deals. They can be rational, even generous. But if your goal is QSBS, secondary purchases are the wrong way to acquire stock *unless* you have a fact pattern that fits into a specific exception or you're relying on a different tax strategy entirely. Most of the time, the simple takeaway is the correct one: buying from another shareholder usually does not create QSBS in the buyer's hands.

If you're negotiating one of these, the most useful question isn't "Is this QSBS?" It's "Is there a way to structure this so the company issues shares instead?" Sometimes the answer is no for business reasons (dilution, approvals, signaling). But at least you'll be negotiating with your eyes open.

"Directly or through an underwriter": why that phrase exists (and where it shows up)

Most startup shareholders will never interact with an underwriter in the way public companies do, but the statutory phrase—acquired at original issuance "directly or through an underwriter"—is still worth respecting. It signals what the law is trying to capture: stock coming into circulation from the company, not from existing holders.

In practice, the "through an underwriter" idea can show up in structured financings where an intermediary plays a formal role in placing shares. That doesn't mean every intermediary or platform is an underwriter, and it doesn't mean your Carta-issued electronic record is "underwriting." It means the law is comfortable with the idea that an issuance can be mediated and still be an issuance. The key is still that the corporation is issuing new shares.

SAFEs and convertible notes: the conversion is where your stock is born

SAFEs and convertible notes are equity-adjacent instruments—useful, popular, and often misunderstood in QSBS conversations precisely because they are not stock until they convert.

When a SAFE or note converts into stock, that conversion is typically the moment you become a stockholder. It's when the corporation issues shares to you. That's why conversions deserve extra scrutiny: they create a new issuance event, often at a time when the company looks very different than it did when you first wired money.

This leads to two practical implications that catch investors off guard:

- *Your QSBS "start date" can be later than your investment date.* You may have felt invested when you signed the SAFE. For QSBS, your clock often starts when you actually receive stock.
- *The company-level tests must be evaluated around that issuance.* A company that was comfortably under thresholds at the seed stage might be in a very different posture at the priced round when the conversion happens. That's not an argument against SAFEs; it's an argument for not being casual about the conversion mechanics.

Also: conversions can be messy in the real world. Documents get amended, rounds get delayed, "post-money" vs "pre-money" SAFE terms change allocations, and sometimes multiple conversions happen across multiple rounds. The law can handle complexity; what it can't handle is an absence of a clear factual record of when shares were issued and under what terms.

Stock for property: plausible, but don't assume "I contributed something" is enough

Original issuance can include stock issued in exchange for property (with statutory limitations). This is relevant when founders contribute intellectual property, equipment, or other assets at formation or shortly after.

The interesting twist is that "property" in founder land can get philosophical fast. Is an idea property? Is a domain name property? Is code property if it was written before incorporation? Sometimes yes, but don't rely on intuition—rely on documents.

The practical QSBS angle is: if you're counting on stock being issued for property, document the contribution like it could be audited. Spell out what was contributed, when it was transferred, and how the company valued it for issuance purposes. The cleaner the paper trail, the less likely QSBS becomes an argument built on vibes and memory.

Reorganizations and transfers: QSBS can survive, but "fact-specific" is not a throwaway phrase

Transfers and corporate transactions can preserve QSBS status and the relevant time period in some cases (tacking concepts), but these are the situations where amateur certainty is dangerous. The corporate lawyer's view ("the shares rolled over") and the tax lawyer's view ("the taxpayer acquired new stock") can diverge in subtle ways.

Common moments that deserve extra attention:

- *Company reorganizations.* Mergers, recapitalizations, or changes in classes of stock can result in old shares being exchanged for new shares. Sometimes the QSBS character carries over; sometimes a particular step breaks it. The answer is often in the exact legal sequence.
- *Gifts and transfers among family vehicles.* Transfers can preserve QSBS character in the hands of the recipient in some circumstances, but you still have to track who the taxpayer is and whether the recipient is positioned to use the exclusion.

- *Entity contributions.* Contributing stock to a partnership, LLC, or corporation can be a governance move, an asset-protection move, or a planning move. It's also a moment where QSBS attributes can be altered or trapped. Treat these like tax events even when they're marketed as "administrative."

The most useful posture is not "I read on a forum that it tacks." The useful posture is: "The sequence matters; show me the documents; show me what the taxpayer actually received."

A document-review habit that pays off: reconstruct the issuance story from the inside out

If you've ever tried to do this after the fact—during a sale process, under time pressure—you know how quickly it turns into a scavenger hunt. The better approach is to build a simple issuance dossier for every meaningful tranche you own. Not a thesis. A file.

For each block of shares that might be QSBS-relevant, you want to be able to answer, with receipts:

- *Was the stock newly issued by the company?* (Not bought from someone else.)
- *What was exchanged for the stock?* (Money, property, or services.)
- *What event actually caused the shares to be issued?* (Formation issuance, option exercise, conversion.)
- *What is the "proof packet"?* (Stock purchase agreement or exercise notice, board consent, proof of payment, cap table entry, and any conversion documents.)

You're not doing this to satisfy bureaucratic instincts. You're doing it because QSBS is a high-dollar claim that often gets reviewed in diligence or challenged in audits, and the cleanest defense is a clean narrative supported by dated documents.

Mixed tranches: one company, multiple QSBS outcomes

Real cap tables are layered. You might have:

- founder shares issued for services,
- exercised option shares issued years later,
- shares acquired in a secondary purchase,
- shares acquired on a SAFE conversion,
- and maybe some shares received in a reorganization.

It's tempting to treat all of that as "my equity." Tax law doesn't. It treats each acquisition pathway as its own story, with its own start date and its own vulnerabilities. That's why people sometimes discover that only *some* of their gain is eligible, or that the shares they assumed were their "best" shares (because they were acquired later at a higher strike price) are the ones with a cleaner original-issuance narrative—while the early shares have gaps in documentation.

The adult move is to map your tranches now, while time is cheap.

A final gut-check before you sign anything involving stock

Any time you're about to acquire shares—whether you're a founder granting yourself stock, an employee exercising, or an investor writing a check—pause long enough to ask one question that sounds too simple to matter:

> *Am I getting stock from the company, or from another shareholder?*

If it's from the company, you're at least in the original-issuance lane (subject to all the other requirements). If it's from another shareholder, assume it's not QSBS in your hands unless a knowledgeable advisor can point to a clear, document-supported reason otherwise.

That one question prevents a huge percentage of QSBS heartbreak—because most heartbreak isn't caused by exotic tax law. It's caused by a normal business deal that accidentally took the only route Section 1202 doesn't like.

3.3 The Company-Level Qualification Tests

QSBS can be perfectly "clean" on the investor side—right taxpayer, right acquisition path, immaculate paperwork—and still fail for one quiet reason: the company wasn't eligible at the exact moment the shares were issued, or it drifted out of compliance while you owned them. That's why sophisticated buyers don't treat QSBS as a personal trait. They treat it as an issuer trait with receipts.

The issuer-side rules are the ones founders usually assume are "handled somewhere in legal." Sometimes they are. Often they're handled in the same way smoke alarms are handled in rentals: everyone assumes someone else checked the batteries.

At a high level, the company must clear three gates: (1) it must be a domestic C corporation for substantially all of the holder's holding period; (2) it must be under the applicable aggregate gross assets ceiling at issuance (tested at specific times around the issuance); and (3) during substantially all of that ownership span, it must use substantially all of its assets in the active conduct of a qualified trade or business—meaning a business that isn't on the excluded list, and that isn't quietly turning into a cash-and-investments holding tank.

Gate 1: It has to be a domestic C corporation (and it has to stay that way)

The cleanest QSBS fact pattern starts with a boring sentence that too many companies can't honestly say: *"We were a domestic C corporation for substantially all of the holder's time in the stock."*

The "C corporation" part sounds like a formation choice, but it's really an identity that must be true over time. Entity classification history is therefore critical—especially for companies that began as LLCs or partnerships, or that made S elections early on. Startups evolve; corporate tax status is less forgiving.

A few ways this goes sideways in practice:

- A company starts life as an LLC "just for speed," then converts later. That can still be a great business decision, but it creates a fault line: the stock doesn't exist until the corporation exists, and any pre-corporate interests aren't QSBS stock.
- A company files an S election, then later revokes it or terminates it. Investors often remember the company "being a corporation," but Section 1202 is explicit about C corporations.
- A company has foreign complexity—an offshore parent, a foreign issuer, or a structure where the entity issuing "equity" is not the domestic operating company. QSBS wants a domestic C corporation issuer.

None of that is inherently disqualifying for building a real company. It's disqualifying for *QSBS on that issuer's stock*. And that's the point: QSBS doesn't reward ambition. It rewards compliance.

If you're doing diligence—on your own company or someone else's—ask for the corporate status timeline the way you'd ask for a cap table: "Show me the formation documents, elections, and conversions, and tell me what the entity was for tax purposes at each point."

Gate 2: The gross-assets test is a snapshot, not a vibe

The gross-assets test is where founders get tripped up by their own success. Everyone can recite the headline—there's a gross-assets ceiling—but the practical hazard is timing. The corporation must be under the applicable aggregate gross assets ceiling at relevant times before and immediately after the issuance.

That language is doing real work. It's telling you the test is not "around the seed stage" or "when we were small." It's a snapshot taken at the issuance moment, with specific "before" and "immediately after" framing. If the company crosses the threshold at the wrong time, shares issued after that snapshot may never be QSBS, even if the company still "feels" small by Silicon Valley standards.

Two counterintuitive points make this test particularly sneaky:

Cap table growth is not the same thing as asset growth

Founders often track valuation and ownership percentages obsessively, but the gross-assets test isn't a valuation test. "We raised at a $300M valuation" doesn't automatically tell you anything about gross assets. Similarly, "we only have 12 employees" doesn't save you if the balance sheet is heavy.

Gross assets is about what the company owns—cash, receivables, equipment, IP booked on the balance sheet, and other assets—measured using tax rules that don't always match your mental model.

Contributed property can be measured at fair market value

Practitioners emphasize that contributed property can be measured at fair market value for this purpose, depending on statutory mechanics. Translation: you can't assume "we transferred IP in, and it had a low book value" keeps you under the line. If the contributed property has real value, it can inflate the asset snapshot even if the accounting treatment feels modest.

This is most relevant in founder-heavy situations: IP assignments at formation, contribution of software, patents, or valuable contracts.

The company may treat those as "just getting organized." The QSBS test may treat them as adding real assets.

Timing games you didn't know you were playing

A classic pattern: a priced round closes, and the company suddenly has a large cash balance. If shares are issued in connection with that round—new preferred stock, option exercises, SAFE conversions happening at closing—the gross-assets test is peeking over the company's shoulder.

It gets more delicate when closings are staggered. You can have a "signing" date and a "closing" date. You can have multiple closings days apart. You can have bridge money that lands right before the priced round. If issuances occur across those dates, some tranches may be tested under a different balance sheet snapshot than others.

In other words, it's possible for two employees to exercise options within the same week and end up with different QSBS outcomes because the company's cash landed on Tuesday and one exercised on Monday. That's not drama; that's how snapshot tests behave.

Gate 3: The active business requirement is a long-term behavior test

The active business requirement is where QSBS stops being a "formation" story and becomes an "operating" story. During substantially all of the ownership span, the corporation must use at least the statutory percentage of assets in the active conduct of a qualified trade or business. The phrasing is deliberately repetitive: it's not enough to be active once. The company has to *keep* being active.

This is the rule that punishes companies for hoarding cash without a plan, pivoting into the wrong revenue model, or slowly drifting from "product company" into "high-end services with a software wrapper."

A few real-world pressure points deserve special attention.

Cash is an asset—and too much "idle" cash creates questions

Cash is not neutral in QSBS land. It sits on the balance sheet, and the active business test asks what the company is doing with its assets. Early-stage companies often have a good story: cash is earmarked for hiring, R&D, inventory, or expansion. That narrative aligns with why venture-backed businesses raise money.

But there's a different story that shows up in later stages: the company becomes operationally profitable, stops investing aggressively, and starts carrying a large cash balance (or worse, a passive investment portfolio). That can create risk under the active business requirement because the company's assets may no longer be "substantially" deployed in active business operations.

This is where founders get blindsided: "We became responsible adults" is not an automatic QSBS-safe transition. Responsible adults sometimes accumulate assets that look passive.

Acquisitions can change the asset mix faster than the org chart changes

A company can stay "active" in spirit while changing its balance sheet in a way that makes the active-business percentages harder to satisfy. Buying real estate, acquiring another business with significant non-operating assets, holding large amounts of non-business property—these can all change the asset mix without any dramatic change in day-to-day product work.

Diligence-minded investors watch this. They ask what the company owns, not just what it sells.

The working capital story has to stay believable

Startups often hold significant cash as working capital—money intended to be used in the business. That's normal. Over time, though, the "we're going to hire soon" story needs to be credible. A company that has been around for a while and holds a huge pile of cash while distributing little and investing little can invite scrutiny. The QSBS regime is built to encourage operating businesses, not miniature investment funds with an office lease.

The practical takeaway is not "never hold cash." It's: if the company's balance sheet starts looking like a treasury department, you should treat QSBS as a living compliance issue, not a box checked years ago.

Qualified trade or business: the excluded list is longer than most founders expect

Even if a company is a domestic C corp and nails the asset snapshot at issuance, Section 1202 still cares about what the company *does*. And §1202(e)(3) contains a detailed list of excluded service fields (and a catch-all "reputation or skill" category) and excluded business types (banking/insurance/financing/leasing/investing, farming, natural resource extraction, hotel/restaurant type businesses).

Founders often skim that list and think, "We're a software company; we're fine." The danger is that modern startups blur lines that the statute draws sharply.

Here are the gray zones that most often create QSBS anxiety:

SaaS that sells a product vs. "software" that sells a person

A subscription SaaS business—customers pay for access to software—usually reads like an operating company selling a product. The value is in the system.

A consultancy can look technologically sophisticated and still be, at its core, a business where revenue depends on key individuals and their expertise. That's where the "reputation or skill" catch-all starts to loom. If the business is effectively selling the time, judgment, or personal brand of a small set of experts—even if those experts use proprietary tooling—then the company's activity might be closer to an excluded services model than founders want to admit.

The tell is not whether you have software. The tell is whether the customer is paying for *the software* or paying for *you*, with software as the delivery mechanism.

Fintech: the product can be qualified while the balance sheet quietly becomes financial

Fintech founders often build real products—payments infrastructure, fraud detection, compliance tooling. Those can look like classic qualified businesses.

But fintech is also the land of "we started as software, then we began holding customer funds, extending credit, taking spreads, or doing financing-like activities." Banking/insurance/financing/leasing/investing are explicitly in the excluded business family. The line between "enabling finance" and "being finance" is where careful classification and counsel matter.

Hospitality and "tech-enabled" real-world businesses

Many modern companies describe themselves as tech companies because they use software. But Section 1202 is not grading you on your tech stack. Hotel/restaurant type businesses are in the excluded list, and plenty of "tech-enabled" concepts still economically behave like hospitality or food service businesses with great software.

Again, the question isn't whether you use technology. It's whether the underlying trade or business fits within qualified lanes.

How the IRS tends to think about this: representations, facts, and the paper trail

IRS Private Letter Rulings illustrate how the IRS restates and applies the requirements and why fact representations/documentation matter (even though PLRs are not binding precedent). The pattern is consistent: the IRS asks for the corporate history, the issuance facts, the asset snapshots, and a plain description of the business—what it actually does, how it earns revenue, and how it uses its assets.

That's a helpful mindset even if you never expect an IRS review. The people who will diligence your QSBS posture at exit—buyers, their tax counsel, your own advisors—tend to ask the same questions. Not because they love paperwork, but because QSBS is a high-stakes claim and the rules are specific.

A company that can answer those questions crisply doesn't just have a better QSBS story. It looks more professionally run.

A diligence checklist you can run without becoming a tax lawyer

Founders and investors often want a single "Are we QSBS?" checkbox. Reality is messier, but the diligence process can still be surprisingly practical if you gather the right artifacts.

- *Corporate status history:* Was the issuer a domestic C corporation for substantially all of the owner's time in the stock? If there were conversions, elections, or reorganizations, what were the effective dates?
- *Gross assets at each issuance:* For each meaningful issuance event (founder issuance, option exercise waves, SAFE/note conversions at a priced round), what did the balance sheet look like right before and immediately after? If property was contributed, what was it and how was it valued?
- *Operational story over time:* Has the company used substantially all of its assets in an active qualified business for substantially

all of the ownership span? If cash balances grew, what was the business plan for that cash? If the company acquired assets or businesses, did that change the asset mix?

- *Business model classification:* Does revenue come primarily from a product (like subscription software), or from services tied to individual expertise? Has the company drifted into excluded fields—especially financing-like activity—or into a model that leans heavily on "reputation or skill"?

If you can answer those questions with documents rather than confidence, you're thinking the way a diligence reviewer thinks. That's the goal. QSBS is generous, but it's not sentimental: it doesn't care how hard you worked, only whether the issuer stayed inside the lines while you owned the stock.

3.4 Redemption Traps and the Per-Issuer Limitation

QSBS has a cruel sense of humor: the things that most often wreck it aren't dramatic frauds or exotic tax shelters. They're "normal" company actions—buying back a few shares, running a small liquidity program, cleaning up the cap table before a financing—followed by an investor discovering at exit that the exclusion they counted on is gone or capped far lower than expected.

Two concepts drive that pain. First, redemptions: the company's own repurchases can poison QSBS around specific issuance dates. Second, the per-issuer limitation: even perfect QSBS has an economic ceiling, measured issuer by issuer, taxpayer by taxpayer. You can do everything right and still run into the cap like a low bridge on a moving truck.

The good news is that both problems are predictable. They're only "surprises" when no one was watching.

Why Congress cared about buybacks (and why you should too)

A redemption is the corporation buying back its own stock. In startup life, that can be a kindness (giving employees liquidity), a cleanup (repurchasing unvested shares from a departing founder), or a strategic move (shrinking the cap table before an IPO). In tax law, it can also look like a scheme: taxpayers cycling stock in and out to manufacture QSBS-eligible shares with minimal real risk.

Congress's response was blunt: if the corporation is repurchasing shares around the time it issues QSBS, the new issuance may not get QSBS treatment. Not "might be scrutinized." Potentially disqualified.

The reason this stings is that redemptions are often handled far from the QSBS conversation. The CFO thinks in cash management. The GC thinks in corporate approvals. The HR team thinks in employee morale. QSBS thinks in windows.

The rule you actually need: redemptions are tested in windows around each issuance

Treasury Reg. §1.1202-2 provides two disqualifying redemption regimes keyed to windows around each issuance date—(1) targeted redemptions involving the taxpayer/related persons in a 4-year window (2 years before through 2 years after issuance), and (2) significant redemptions by the corporation from any shareholder in a 2-year window (1 year before through 1 year after issuance) if they exceed specified thresholds.

That sentence is dense, but it's also a roadmap. The most important practical insight is hidden in the phrase "keyed to windows around each issuance date." QSBS is not a single company-wide blessing. It's tranche-sensitive. Each issuance has its own danger zone.

And because redemptions can disqualify a particular issuance (tranche) rather than the entire cap table, a single buyback event can poison shares issued near the repurchase while leaving earlier/later issuances intact (timing-driven). That can lead to bizarre outcomes where two shareholders in the same financing round have different QSBS status because their shares were technically issued on different dates, or because one exercised options during the window and the other didn't.

If you want a single mental model: redemptions don't just reduce outstanding shares. They cast a shadow forward and backward in time.

Targeted redemptions: the "you (or your relatives) got bought out" problem

The targeted regime is personal. It focuses on redemptions involving the taxpayer or related persons around the issuance.

This catches scenarios that feel innocuous in founder culture:

- *Founder departure cleanup.* A departing founder sells back stock to the company, the company reissues stock to a new hire or new investor, and everyone calls it "cap table hygiene." That redemption can be close enough to the issuance to create a QSBS issue for the new shares.
- *Family reshuffling.* Shares move among family members and family vehicles, and the company repurchases some portion from one member. Related-person rules can pull transactions together in ways that surprise non-tax folks.
- *"Small" repurchases that feel beneath notice.* A company buys back a little stock from an employee every quarter. One quarter doesn't look like anything; the window aggregates behavior in a way that can become meaningful.

The emotional trap here is that founders often treat repurchases as a private arrangement: "We're just resolving someone's equity." QSBS treats it as a corporate action with consequences for other shareholders' tax attributes.

Significant redemptions: the "the company did a buyback program" problem

The second regime is broader. It looks at significant redemptions by the corporation from *any* shareholder within that 2-year window (1 year before through 1 year after issuance), if they exceed specified thresholds.

This is the one that can blindside a seemingly unrelated investor. You might not have sold a single share back to the company. But if the company repurchased enough stock from others, the issuance you received during the window can be tainted.

Two common startup patterns trigger anxiety here:

- *Liquidity events that are technically redemptions.* Sometimes a "tender" is structured as the company buying shares rather than an outside buyer. The optics are similar—employees sell stock, employees get cash—but the tax mechanics can be different.
- *Pre-financing cleanups.* Companies sometimes repurchase shares from ex-employees or consolidate stray holders right around a financing. That's exactly when new shares are being issued. The overlap is where problems breed.

This is also why "QSBS diligence" isn't just checking a box at formation. If the company is doing anything that looks like a repurchase program, the dates matter as much as the dollar amounts.

The founder liquidity program example: death by a thousand helpful buybacks

Imagine a company that wants to be kind and orderly. It allows employees to sell a small number of shares back to the company each quarter at a board-approved price. It feels controlled. It feels mature. It also creates a recurring redemption stream.

Now layer in reality: the company is still issuing stock too—new hires exercising, refresh grants being exercised, perhaps a SAFE conversion happening at a priced round. Each of those issuances has a redemption window around it, and the company's ongoing repurchases can overlap those windows repeatedly.

The risk isn't just one big repurchase. The risk is that cumulative repurchases cross thresholds, and suddenly a tranche you care about—issued right in the middle of "routine" repurchases—has a QSBS problem.

If you're a founder or CFO, the takeaway isn't "never repurchase shares." It's "treat repurchases like they have a tax blast radius." Keep a redemption log with dates, amounts, and counterparties. When you're about to issue new stock in size (or when lots of option exercises are expected), check the log before you congratulate yourself on clean governance.

Tender offers near a financing: the two transactions that love to collide

Another classic: a company raises a new round and, alongside it, wants to offer some liquidity to employees. Everyone is happy: new money comes in, some longtime team members can pay off loans or buy a home, and the board gets a retention win.

If the company repurchases more than a meaningful amount of stock within the 1-year-before/1-year-after window for a new investor issuance, you can create broad redemption risk for that new issuance. The irony is painful: the financing round that made the company "more real" can simultaneously make the QSBS profile of newly issued shares less reliable.

The practical approach is coordination. If the company is planning both an issuance and a repurchase, those teams need to talk to each other. Not at the level of "is liquidity good for morale," but at the level of "what are the dates, and who is buying from whom?"

Redemptions don't just hit investors—employees exercising can get caught in the crossfire

Founders often think redemption rules are an investor concern. They're not. Employees who exercise options are literally receiving newly issued shares from the corporation. If the company is running repurchases around that time—buying back stock from departing employees, doing small liquidity events—then exercises that occur during the affected window are potential QSBS landmines.

That means the QSBS posture of employee stock can vary by exercise date. Two colleagues with identical option grants can end up in different places simply because one exercised during a repurchase-heavy window and the other exercised later.

This is one of those moments where tax law feels unfair. It's also one of the few moments where a company can make a real difference with process: educate employees on timing sensitivity, avoid stacking repurchases on top of heavy exercise periods, and keep records robust enough that the company can at least explain what happened.

Now the second half of the punchline: even perfect QSBS is capped per issuer

Suppose you clear every eligibility gate. The stock was issued correctly. The company stayed qualified. No redemption windows were violated. You sell at a huge gain.

You still don't get an unlimited exclusion. The per-issuer limitation caps the exclusion for each taxpayer with respect to each issuer as the greater of (a) the applicable dollar cap (which varies by acquisition date under the expanded regime described in post-2025 explanations) or (b) 10× the aggregate adjusted basis of QSBS sold during the taxable year.

This is where QSBS stops being purely legal and becomes explicitly mathematical. It's also where two investors can look at the same exit and experience completely different outcomes because their basis—

what they paid or recognized as investment in the stock—is different.

The two caps: dollar cap vs. 10× basis (and why basis can be destiny)

Most readers instinctively gravitate to the dollar cap: "I can exclude up to $X of gain per issuer." That's intuitive and easy to plan around.

The 10× basis alternative is trickier but often more powerful for certain investors. It says, roughly: if you put in meaningful basis, you can potentially exclude a multiple of that basis—again, issuer by issuer, and based on the aggregate adjusted basis of QSBS sold during the taxable year.

That framing immediately explains a common founder frustration: basis planning matters. Low-basis founder stock often makes the 10× basis rule less helpful, while cash/property contributions that create higher basis can increase the 10× cap (subject to many other tax rules).

Founders often have spectacular paper gains and tiny basis. That's why the basis multiple can feel irrelevant for them and extremely relevant for cash investors.

The important emotional shift is to stop thinking "QSBS equals unlimited tax-free exit." It's "QSBS equals a powerful exclusion, up to the cap that applies to *this taxpayer* for *this issuer*."

Vintage tracking: why issuance date now controls more than you want it to

Recent legislative explanations (e.g., JCT materials) describe post-July 4, 2025 changes, including inflation indexing and higher ceilings for post-enactment stock—making "vintage tracking" (by issuance date) essential.

This creates a practical problem that didn't used to be as sharp: a single person can hold multiple tranches in the same company with different acquisition dates, potentially under different regimes. Option exercises, SAFE conversions, follow-on investments—each can create a new "vintage" of stock.

That's not theoretical. It's day-to-day startup behavior. The tax consequence is that you need to know which shares were acquired when, and you need to track how much per-issuer exclusion capacity you've already used under that issuer across prior sales.

The "prior excluded gain" surprise: your earlier partial liquidity can shrink your later win

Per-issuer limits aren't just about the exit. They're also about your history with that issuer. If you sold some shares earlier—maybe a small liquidity event, maybe a secondary sale—and you claimed QSBS on that gain, that claimed amount doesn't vanish. It lives in your per-issuer ledger. Later, when the big acquisition happens, you may have less remaining capacity than your spreadsheet assumes.

This is where startup life collides with tax life. Startup life treats partial liquidity as a footnote: "I sold a little in 2022, but the real exit is coming." Tax life treats it as: "You used some of your per-issuer exclusion capacity in 2022, so update the running total."

The fix is not complicated; it's just rarely done: maintain an issuer-by-issuer QSBS tracker.

Build the tracker like a grown-up: issuer-by-issuer, tranche-by-tranche

If you only do one operational thing to protect your QSBS outcome, do this: create a simple spreadsheet (or memo) that you update any time you buy, exercise, convert, transfer, or sell.

For each issuer, track:

- *Each acquisition event:* date, number of shares, how acquired (issuance, exercise, conversion), and cost/basis.

- *Each sale event:* date, shares sold, gain realized, and how much QSBS exclusion you claimed (if any).
- *Redemption exposure notes:* whether the company did any repurchases near your issuance dates that deserve review.
- *Remaining per-issuer capacity:* a running view of how much dollar-cap room remains and whether the 10× basis alternative is relevant based on what you've sold in a given year.

Notice what's missing: vibes. This is not a "do we think we qualify" dashboard. It's an evidence log. If you ever find yourself saying, "I'm pretty sure those shares were QSBS," the log is already doing its job by revealing that you don't actually know.

Why this is worth the hassle: redemption risk and cap math compound

Redemption traps and per-issuer limits are annoying on their own. Together, they create a particularly nasty outcome: you can end up with less eligible QSBS than you expected *and* a smaller cap than you assumed on what remains.

For example, if a redemption disqualifies a later tranche—say, shares issued on a SAFE conversion at a priced round—then the tranche you're left relying on may be your earliest, lowest-basis stock. Great for gain size, less great for making the 10× basis alternative meaningful. Meanwhile, any prior partial liquidity you took from that same issuer may have already used up part of the dollar cap. That's how a nine-figure outcome can still produce a surprisingly taxable result, even with "QSBS" in the story.

The core habit is unglamorous: treat company repurchases as tax-sensitive events, and treat per-issuer exclusion capacity as something you can spend down over time. QSBS isn't just about winning the legal argument at the end. It's about not accidentally burning the fuel mid-flight.

Chapter 4

The Expanded 2025 Rules and the New Timing Playbook

For years, QSBS planning often felt like a long, patient countdown to a single five-year finish line. The 2025 changes break that old rhythm. Now the date your stock is issued can change the rules, shorter holding periods may unlock partial benefits, and companies that once looked too large may still fit inside the tent. This chapter shows readers how to stop treating QSBS as a static tax label and start using it as a timing strategy.

4.1 Why Issuance Date Became a First-Order Variable

The sneakiest QSBS mistake in 2025 isn't a missed form or a forgotten signature. It's a story founders and early investors tell themselves because it feels tidy: "*I own stock in the company. Therefore all of my stock is basically the same.*" That story used to be only mildly dangerous. After the July 4, 2025 changeover, it's a category error. Two blocks of shares in the *same* startup—held by the *same* person—can live under different QSBS benefit structures simply because they were issued on different dates. You don't fix that later with a clever spreadsheet; you fix it now with clean "vintage" tracking.

The practical consequence is surprisingly emotional. When a buyer shows up with a term sheet, you want the tax answer to be a single sentence: "My gain is excludable." Instead, you may be staring at three different tranches of the same company's stock, each with its own rules, its own clock, and potentially its own cap. Your banker will call it "one position." Your cap table will show "one line." The IRS will not.

The post-2025 world rewards a habit that feels boring until it saves you seven figures: treat stock like wine. Same winery, different vintages. A founder grant from early days, shares picked up later through an employee plan, and a follow-on angel check can be three distinct vintages. Each vintage has its own acquisition date and its own QSBS regime. Blend them together and you'll accidentally claim the best rule for the whole pile—exactly the sort of "reasonable misunderstanding" that becomes very unreasonable during diligence.

Here's the reason issuance date now sits at the top of the decision tree. As of July 4, 2025, Congress effectively created a second QSBS regime. Stock issued on or before that date generally keeps the older structure; stock issued after that date can qualify for the expanded benefits (the new tiered schedule and the larger cap, assuming everything else checks out). That split means the first question for any modeling exercise is no longer "Do I have QSBS?" It's "*Which* QSBS regime applies to *this block* of stock?" The answer depends on issuance timing, not your job title, not your intent, not the company's pitch deck.

This is where otherwise meticulous founders get tripped up: a cap table is designed to explain *ownership*, not *tax*. It's a map of *who has what* today, not a diary of *how and when each person got it*. QSBS cares about the diary. If you wait until an exit is on the calendar to reconstruct it, you'll discover that "we can probably find that" is an expensive phrase—because the proof you need lives in board consents, exercise notices, subscription agreements, and payment records that were never built to be charming twenty-five minutes before an acquisition call.

A good way to feel the problem is to picture three common characters at the same startup:

The founder got common stock at formation. That block may be under the older regime because it was issued years before 2025.

The early employee received options in 2024, then exercised some in late 2025 after a promotion and a refreshed belief in the company. The option grant date is not the stock date (as we saw earlier), so the shares from that exercise are a later vintage—possibly under the expanded regime.

The angel investor bought shares in a seed round in 2023, then added more in a SAFE conversion or a priced round in 2026. Even if both purchases were "early," they are not the same vintage for QSBS. The second check may be better (new cap, tiered schedule) or worse (asset threshold issues at issuance), but it is definitely *different*.

In conversation, everyone calls these "my shares." For planning, they are three separate stacks.

The hardest part is accepting that issuance date isn't just a date field; it's a switch. It determines which benefit structure the stock is even *allowed* to seek. That changes behavior. It changes how you react to a late-year financing. It changes whether you rush to exercise before a holiday or you wait. It changes whether you treat a founder refresh grant as "just more stock" or as a distinct tax asset that deserves its own folder and its own memo while the facts are still warm.

So what counts as a new issuance event in real life? Not in an academic way—in the messy way equity actually moves inside startups.

A purchase in a financing round is the cleanest example. You sign, you wire money, the company issues shares to you. That block has an issuance date tied to that closing.

An employee's stock purchase from exercising a right to buy shares is also a new issuance. The moment the company issues the shares to you—after a valid exercise and payment—creates a new vintage. It doesn't matter that you've "been here since 2022." The stock didn't exist in your hands until the issuance.

A conversion that results in stock being issued (for example, when a convertible instrument converts into shares) can create a new issuance event. The critical point for your records isn't the romance of the original check; it's the date the corporation issued stock and to whom. Conversions can also create multiple vignettes inside one story: one instrument, one conversion, stock issued on one date, but allocated across different taxpayers if the instrument was transferred or held through entities. The story is simple; the paperwork is not.

A gift or inheritance doesn't create a new issuance by the corporation—but it creates a new *taxpayer owner* and often a new recordkeeping problem. QSBS exclusions are computed at the taxpayer level. If shares move from you to a spouse, child, or trust, the dates and rules may carry in particular ways, but the computation and proof obligations don't magically stay with the original holder. The corporation didn't issue new stock, yet your planning needs a fresh file because the person claiming the exclusion is different.

A secondary purchase is the classic false friend. You "bought stock," sure. But you bought it from someone else, not from the company. The issuance date of those shares is the original issuance date (and the original issuance requirement still governs whether the buyer can claim QSBS). So secondary trades don't create a helpful new post-2025 vintage; they usually create a documentation headache stapled to someone else's long-forgotten issuance.

There are also events that feel like issuance events but usually aren't. A stock split, for example, changes the number of shares but generally doesn't create a new purchase. A reclassification from one class to another might not reset your vintage, but it can complicate basis and documentation. Treat these as "stop and document" moments even if they aren't "new issuance" moments; they are the exact times your later self will wish you wrote down what happened while everyone still remembered.

Board approvals matter here in the same way notarization matters on a deed: you can own the house without a fancy story, but you can't sell it cleanly if the paperwork is a mystery. Stock issuances are corporate acts. A proper issuance normally has a board consent (or minutes), an issuance notice or stock purchase agreement, and proof of consideration (cash paid, services rendered, or a net exercise). If those documents are missing, you can still have valid ownership under state law depending on the facts, but you've made your future QSBS proof unnecessarily fragile.

Exercise confirmations deserve their own paragraph because they're the most common point of "I thought that was the date." Many startups treat the exercise flow as an HR-adjacent task: a PDF, a wire, a counter-signature. From a QSBS standpoint, that's a moment of birth for a new vintage of stock. If you ever exercised in chunks—some early for AMT planning, some later for risk reasons—you may have multiple small vintages. That's not a nuisance; it's optionality. The only tragedy is losing that optionality because you can't prove the dates.

If this sounds like obsessive recordkeeping, good. QSBS is one of the few places in the tax code where "boring compliance" can turn into a life-changing outcome. And the expanded 2025 rules increase the payoff for getting the details right, because the gap between one vintage and another can be enormous: different exclusion percentages at different times, different dollar limitations, different planning around how long you keep the shares. None of that works if you treat your ownership like a smoothie.

A useful way to organize your thinking is to stop saying "my company stock" and start saying "my blocks of company stock." A block is defined by (1) how you acquired it, (2) when it was issued to you, and (3) who the taxpayer is. Once you do that, a lot of confusing questions become clean.

For example: "Do I qualify for the new post-2025 benefits?" is not a single question. It's three questions:

- Which blocks were issued after July 4, 2025?
- For those blocks, what is the holding clock for *that* block?
- For those blocks, did the company meet the gross-assets test at the moment *those* shares were issued?

Notice what's missing: none of those questions can be answered from memory alone. They are records questions.

There's another subtle benefit to block thinking: it forces you to confront the difference between a company narrative and a tax narrative. Company narrative is: "We started in a garage, then raised a seed, then a Series A." Tax narrative is: "On these dates, the corporation issued shares to these taxpayers for this consideration, and on those dates the corporation's gross assets were below the relevant threshold." Those are not the same story, even when they describe the same business. QSBS lives in the tax narrative.

The post-2025 split also changes how you should talk to your co-founder, your CFO, and your lawyer. Before, if someone asked "Are we a QSBS company?" you could treat it like a brand label. Now, the only safe answer is more specific: "We have a QSBS analysis, and we track eligibility at each issuance." That sounds fussy, but it's the difference between a helpful corporate policy and an awkward scramble where everyone emails the same overstretched finance lead for a number they never had.

Founders feel this most acutely when they do something perfectly normal: they grant themselves additional shares later. A founder refresh grant can be a smart governance move—realigning incentives, fixing early imbalances, or recognizing that the company you have now is not the company you had at formation. But it is not "more of the same" stock. It's a new issuance date, potentially a new QSBS regime, potentially a different basis, and therefore a different planning asset. Even if every other QSBS requirement is met, you can't claim a post-2025 benefit on pre-2025 shares by wishing; you can only do it by owning shares actually issued after the effective date and meeting the requirements for those shares.

Employees face a different flavor of the problem: staggered equity. Many employees accumulate a mosaic—an early exercise here, a later exercise there, a small restricted stock purchase, then perhaps shares from a later equity incentive. That mosaic can be a feature, not a bug. It means you may be able to sell some shares earlier with less tax benefit while keeping another block longer for more benefit, aligning taxes with life needs. But that flexibility only exists if the blocks are distinguishable. If your records are blurred, every sale becomes an argument with your own spreadsheet.

Investors have their own version: "I invested early" is not a QSBS category. Investors often invest in multiple rounds, sometimes through different vehicles, sometimes through an entity, sometimes directly. Each closing is a separate issuance. Each issuance has its own eligibility at issuance. Each issuance has its own holding clock. If you're an angel who writes checks with the same casual ease you order coffee, you still need one unsexy discipline: keep a *deal folder* that includes the stock purchase agreement or subscription agreement, proof of payment, and whatever the company provides about its QSBS status at that time. When the exit comes, your future self will thank your past self for being slightly less chill.

A quick word about "clean records," because that phrase can sound like an accountant's vague scolding. Clean records are not a mountain of PDFs. They're a short set of facts that can be proven quickly:

- the date the shares were issued to you (not when you first joined, not when you first cared)
- the number and class of shares

- your basis (what you paid or what was treated as paid)
- the taxpayer owner (you, spouse, trust, partnership, IRA—whichever is actually claiming the exclusion)

That's the spine. Everything else is backup.

If you want to be slightly more sophisticated (and you do, if your upside is meaningful), add one more field: *how* the shares were acquired. "Founder issuance for services," "cash purchase in seed," "employee purchase via exercise," "conversion," "gift." That acquisition pathway is often what triggers special rules, special holding-period nuances, or special diligence questions. It also helps a CPA review your file without playing detective.

A share ledger doesn't need to be fancy. A single table—kept by you, not just by the company—can prevent most QSBS self-sabotage. The company's cap table is necessary, but it isn't designed to track your personal tax basis, your transfers, or your proof of payment. Build your own "personal cap table" that mirrors reality from your perspective.

Here's a simple template that works for founders, employees, and angels. If you keep it updated, almost every later conversation becomes easier: your tax modeling, your estate planning, your discussions with a buyer's diligence team, and your own decisions about when to sell.

Block ID	*Issuer*	*Issue Date*	*Shares*	*Basis*	*Acquisition Path*
A1	Startup, Inc.	2023-02-10	2,000,000	$2,000	Founder issuance (services/purchase)
B1	Startup, Inc.	2025-11-18	50,000	$25,000	Employee stock purchase (exercise)
C1	Startup, Inc.	2026-06-30	100,000	$100,000	Cash purchase (priced round)

Table 4.1: A personal QSBS block ledger: keep your shares separated by issuance date and acquisition path.

Add a second small table (or extra columns) if you use multiple taxpayers. QSBS is claimed by the taxpayer, and planning strategies often involve spouses or trusts. If you later transfer shares, don't overwrite history—create a new line that reflects the new owner and the transfer date, and preserve the original block detail. Think "audit trail," not "current state."

If you're wondering how precise this needs to be: precise enough that, five years from now, a stranger with a checklist could follow it. Exit diligence is often performed by professionals who have never met you and do not have your emotional attachment to your story. They will ask for dates. They will ask for documents. They will not accept "approximately."

There's also a timing trap that hides inside "issuance date": internal administrative delays. Startups sometimes approve grants on one date, issue on another, and upload everything to a portal on a third. When the benefits hinge on being on one side of a statutory line, you want the legally effective issuance date supported by the corporate records—not the day Carta emailed you or the day you found it in your inbox. If you're close to an effective date and the company is moving slowly, politely insist on clarity. In a world of dual QSBS regimes, "we'll backdate it" is not a casual suggestion; it's a red flag with consequences.

Another practical point: you can't do this exercise once and forget it. The right rhythm is "update on every equity event." Every time you sign something involving equity—grant, purchase, exercise, conversion, transfer—add a row or update a row in your personal ledger and drop the supporting PDF into a dedicated folder. If you do it in real time, it takes ten minutes. If you do it during acquisition talks, it becomes a multi-week archaeology project with your attorney billing by the hour and your spouse asking why you look haunted.

To make this immediately actionable, here's a checklist you can run *this week*—not to become a tax expert, but to make sure you're not missing the raw ingredients needed for QSBS planning under the expanded 2025 rules.

- Create a folder (cloud or local) titled "QSBS — [Company Name]."
- Export or screenshot your current holdings from the cap table portal, but treat it as a reference, not a final answer.
- Gather every document that created stock in your hands: founder purchase docs, stock purchase agreements, exercise notices, conversion confirmations, and proof of payment (wire confirmations or canceled checks).
- Build your personal block ledger with one row per issuance event.
- For each row, note: issue date, shares, class, basis, acquisition path, and taxpayer owner.
- Flag any row where you cannot prove the issue date from a corporate document. That's your "fix it while you still can" list.
- If you have multiple blocks around mid-2025 or later, label them explicitly as "pre-July 4, 2025" or "post-July 4, 2025" vintages so you don't accidentally blend regimes in a future spreadsheet.

That last bullet may feel almost childish—color-coding your shares by a calendar date. But it's exactly the kind of simple guardrail that prevents expensive mistakes. When your ownership includes multiple vintages, the default human impulse is to average everything. QSBS does not average. It separates.

Once you've done this sorting, the rest of the QSBS analysis becomes dramatically cleaner. You'll be able to ask the right questions in the right order, and your advisors will be able to answer them without guessing. More importantly, you'll be able to make timing decisions with your eyes open—because you'll know which shares are playing by which set of rules, and you'll stop accidentally treating your equity like one undifferentiated pile of "startup stock."

4.2 The Tiered Holding Period Schedule After 2025

For years, QSBS timing had the drama of a single trapdoor: five years or nothing (at least nothing that felt worth bragging about). That created a particular startup psychology. Everyone stared at the same date on the calendar, and any exit that arrived early—especially one that arrived at year four and change—felt like a tax tragedy.

Stock issued after July 4, 2025 changes the rhythm. The benefit is no longer a cliff; it's a set of ledges. Reach the first ledge and you may exclude *some* of the gain. Stay on the wall longer and you can exclude more. The commonly used shorthand is simple and surprisingly powerful: for post-effective-date stock, 50% exclusion after 3 years, 75% after 4 years, and 100% after 5+ years. Pre-effective-date stock still lives in the older world, where exiting before five years usually means you don't get the big federal payoff.

That shift does something subtle to your negotiating posture. Under the old regime, if an acquirer wanted to close two months before your five-year mark, your tax outcome often looked the same as closing fourteen months early: *no QSBS exclusion*. Under the new regime for post-2025 shares, two months can be the difference between 50% and 75% (or 75% and 100%) of the gain being excluded. When the "extra" benefit is measured in millions, you stop treating time like an inconvenience and start treating it like a term.

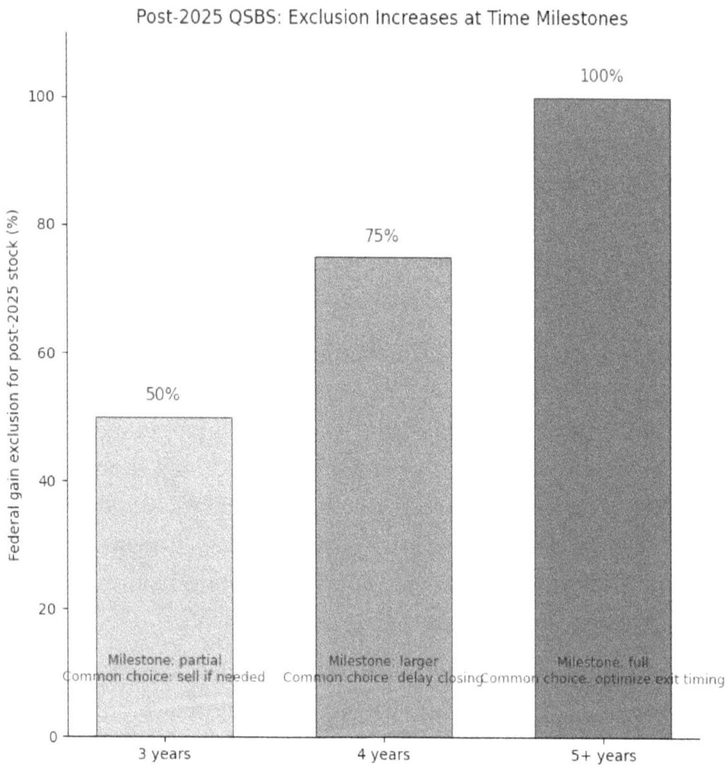

The tiered schedule creates a new kind of conversation inside companies: not "Are we past five years yet?" but "Which milestone is closest for *this block of shares*, and what does one more year buy us?" That sounds like spreadsheet talk until you translate it into something more human—after-tax dollars you can use for a house, financial independence, or diversifying out of a single-risk asset.

A quick illustration with round numbers (not a promise; just a way to see the stakes). Assume:

- You sell post-2025 QSBS with $10 million of gain.
- Your effective combined federal capital gains and net investment income tax rate is 23.8% (20% + 3.8%).

At the 3-year milestone, a 50% exclusion means $5 million is taxable; the federal tax on that slice is about $1.19 million. At 4 years, a 75% exclusion means $2.5 million is taxable; tax is about $595k. At 5+ years, a 100% exclusion means $0 taxable federally; tax is $0. Put differently: that fourth year can be worth roughly $595k of federal savings in this simplified example, and the fifth-year milestone can be worth another $595k. When your gain is larger—or your state taxes don't cooperate—those numbers can get loud quickly.

This is why "waiting one more year" becomes a real decision rather than a vague aspiration. You're not waiting for an abstract tax benefit. You're waiting for a specific rung on a ladder.

The new skill: measuring time like the IRS does

The tiered schedule makes sloppy date tracking more expensive. When five years was the lone gate, many owners treated the date as approximate. "I exercised around fall of 2021." "The seed round was summer 2020." Approximations are the enemy of milestone-based benefits. When the difference between 3 years and 4 years is an extra 25% exclusion, "around" becomes a dangerous word.

As you saw earlier, the clock starts with the issuance event for the block of stock you're selling—not when you signed an offer letter, not when you first started "earning" equity psychologically, and not when you got serious about taxes. For employees, the most common mismatch is assuming the clock began when the option was granted; for investors, it's assuming the clock began with a SAFE signing rather than when shares were actually issued; for founders, it's forgetting that additional grants later create new clocks. The tiered regime doesn't introduce that concept, but it dramatically increases the reward for respecting it.

A practical way to think about the measurement problem is this: milestone planning turns dates into deal terms. If you're negotiating an acquisition, the buyer will care about purchase price, escrow, reps, and indemnities. You should care about *closing date* with the same seriousness when you're within striking distance of a milestone for post-2025 shares. A "quick close" can be a hidden haircut; a slightly delayed close can be a tax raise.

Three real-world timing decisions (and how to think about them)

The tiered schedule doesn't eliminate hard choices. It just replaces the old binary with a set of more nuanced trade-offs. In practice, most owners end up choosing among three paths: sell now, wait for a better tier, or roll into new QSBS when the timing is close but not quite there.

Choice 1: Sell now (and take the tier you've earned)

Sometimes the best financial move is the boring one: take liquidity when it's on the table. A 50% exclusion at three years can still be a big deal—especially if you're sitting on concentrated risk, dealing with burnout, or staring at a life event that doesn't care about your tax calendar.

The underappreciated benefit of the new tier is psychological: it reduces regret. Under the older regime, selling at year 3.5 could feel like "I threw away QSBS." Under the post-2025 schedule, selling at year 3.5 can still capture a meaningful federal benefit. You're not empty-handed; you're simply not at the top rung yet.

When does "sell now" tend to win?

- Your liquidity need is real, not theoretical (taxes, housing, family, diversification).
- The offer price already bakes in peak optimism, and waiting exposes you to downside that dwarfs the additional exclusion.
- Your company risk has shifted from "execution risk" to "financing risk," where one bad macro quarter can change everything.

This is also the moment to remember mixed-vintage ownership. You might sell the block that has reached a milestone while holding a different block longer, depending on the deal structure and what you're allowed to do. Many owners never consider that because they think they have "one" holding clock. You don't—unless you refuse to do the paperwork.

Choice 2: Wait for a better tier (and treat the calendar as money)

Waiting sounds easy in theory: do nothing, pay less tax later. In reality, waiting is an active choice to keep risk on your balance sheet. The question isn't "Is a bigger exclusion good?" Of course it is. The question is whether the incremental after-tax benefit is worth the incremental time exposed to company-specific risk.

Here's a clean way to frame it: calculate the *tax delta* between tiers, then compare it to the *risk cost* of waiting.

Using the earlier simplified assumption of a 23.8% federal rate, each extra 25% of gain excluded saves about 5.95% of total gain (0.25 × 23.8%). On a $10 million gain, that's roughly $595k per step. On a $30 million gain, it's about $1.785 million per step. That is real money—but it is not infinite money.

Now ask what you're risking for that step:

- A down-round that compresses your price
- A missed product transition
- A competitive shock
- A change in the buyer's strategic priorities
- Your own time and attention (which is not free, even if it doesn't show up in a model)

A founder approached at 3 years and 10 months is the classic "calendar as money" situation for post-2025 shares. If you can negotiate a delayed closing, a longer signing-to-closing gap, or a structure where the taxable event occurs after the milestone, the incremental benefit may justify real effort. But don't treat this as a moral crusade. Treat it like any other term: you're asking the buyer for value (time) in exchange for value (deal certainty, price movement, or concessions elsewhere).

Employees face a different version at around 4 years. An employee with a concentrated net worth in company stock is often less worried about squeezing the last basis point out of taxes and more worried about the idea that one company can rewrite their financial life. The tiered schedule is helpful because it lets them quantify the reward for waiting versus the cost of staying concentrated. It turns "I think I should diversify" into "Waiting 11 more months might save roughly $X; is that worth the concentration risk?"

Choice 3: Use a rollover strategy when timing is close but not ideal

Sometimes the deal arrives early and you can't move it. Maybe the buyer wants a fast close. Maybe the company is running out of runway and needs certainty. Maybe you're in a process and time is the enemy. In those cases, the new tiered schedule may still leave real tax on the table—especially if you're under three years for post-2025 shares, or if you're holding pre-2025 stock that doesn't get a partial benefit.

That's when a Section 1045 rollover often enters the conversation. The concept is simple: under certain rules, you can sell QSBS before reaching the full benefit and reinvest the proceeds into new QSBS within the required window, potentially deferring gain. It's not a magic wand, and it's not always available depending on your facts, but it exists for exactly the emotional moment founders dread: "The exit is happening before the best tax outcome."

A few practical points keep expectations realistic:

- A rollover is usually about *deferral,* not immediate exclusion. You're pushing the tax problem forward by swapping into new qualifying stock rather than paying now.
- The reinvestment has to be done carefully and quickly, and it narrows your investment universe at the moment you may want maximum flexibility.
- Rolling into new QSBS reintroduces company risk—you've traded one concentrated bet for another, even if you diversify across multiple qualifying investments.

The tiered schedule changes how rollover thinking shows up. Before, the emotional pitch for a rollover often sounded like: "Do this or lose QSBS entirely." Now it can sound like: "You're at 50% or 75% excluded, but if you want to preserve the remaining upside of a full exclusion, consider whether a rollover makes sense for the taxable slice." That's a different, more surgical use of the tool.

Mixed-vintage exits: one company, two clocks, two answers

The tiered regime creates an odd but increasingly common outcome: one exit, multiple federal tax answers for the same seller.

Imagine you own two blocks in the same startup:

- Block A was issued before July 4, 2025 (older regime).
- Block B was issued after July 4, 2025 (new tiered regime).

At 4 years from Block B's issuance, Block B might be eligible for a 75% exclusion (assuming other requirements are met). Block A, even if you've held it for 4 years too, may still be stuck waiting for the five-year gate under the older structure. If you sell both blocks in the same transaction, you can't "average" your way to a single exclusion percentage. Each block gets its own outcome.

That's not merely a compliance annoyance. It can change what you do with the deal:

- You might negotiate to sell one block now and retain another block longer (if the buyer allows rollover equity or a retained stake).
- You might push for an earnout or milestone payment that triggers later (though earnouts have their own complexities).
- You might treat the transaction as a chance to clean up your shareholder base: sell the less favorable block and keep the block with better tax economics.

None of those are universally "right." The point is that the tiered schedule turns timing into something you can actually *use*, but only if you respect the block-by-block reality.

A decision framework that doesn't pretend you live in a spreadsheet

Tax strategy is often presented as if your life's only variable is the tax rate. Real decisions are messier. The tiered schedule is powerful, but it's still just one input. A useful framework weighs four forces:

After-tax delta. Quantify the incremental savings from moving from 50% to 75% to 100% exclusion for the block(s) affected. If you can't estimate it within 10 minutes, you don't yet have the right records.

Liquidity pressure. Is this "nice to have" cash or "need to have" cash? Your mortgage doesn't accept a promise of future tax optimization.

Business risk. What is the probability-weighted downside of waiting? If the next year includes major product risk, regulatory risk, or financing risk, that matters. If the company is already in a low-volatility, high-visibility phase, waiting may be less painful.

Plan B mechanics. If you can't or won't wait, is there a rollover path worth exploring for the taxable slice? Even when the answer is "no," checking can prevent you from leaving an option unexamined.

This framework has one hidden superpower: it forces you to separate what's controllable from what isn't. You can sometimes negotiate closing timing. You can choose whether to sign a tender or roll equity. You can plan for cash needs. You cannot control the macro cycle, a buyer's board, or the competitive landscape. The tiered schedule rewards owners who control what they can without becoming religious about what they can't.

Where timing gets slippery: closings, installments, and reality

Milestones sound clean until you remember how deals actually close. A transaction can be signed in one month and close in another. Proceeds can be paid over time. Part of the consideration can be escrowed. You might roll some equity into the buyer. Each of these can affect when gain is recognized and how much gain is recognized at each time.

The tiered schedule makes those details more valuable to understand, because "when is my taxable event?" can be worth more than "what is my price?" at the margins. Two deals with the same headline valuation can produce different after-tax outcomes if one pays cash at close and the other pays half now and half later, or if one closes just before a milestone and the other closes just after.

That doesn't mean you should obsess over every structure nuance on your own. It does mean you should stop treating dates as a footnote. When you are within a year of a milestone for post-2025 shares, the timeline belongs in the same conversation as price, escrow, and employment terms.

A compact way to track milestones by block

Because the new schedule is milestone-based, it helps to maintain a "milestone dashboard" alongside your block ledger. Nothing fancy—just a simple table that turns issue dates into milestone dates. If you have multiple blocks, this will quickly reveal where you have near-term leverage and where you don't.

Block ID	*Issue Date*	*3-year date*	*4-year date*	*5-year date*
B1	2025-11-18	2028-11-18	2029-11-18	2030-11-18
C1	2026-06-30	2029-06-30	2030-06-30	2031-06-30

Table 4.2: Milestone dates for post-2025 blocks: a simple dashboard that turns timing into a usable planning input.

This table becomes especially useful when your company is "exit-adjacent"—strong inbound interest, bankers circling, competitors consolidating. It keeps you from being surprised by your own calendar.

The expanded 2025 rules didn't make QSBS effortless. They made it *negotiable*. The exclusion is now something you can approach in stages, and each stage has a clear economic value. That's a gift, but it's also a demand: you have to know which stock is on the new schedule, you have to know the dates precisely, and you have to treat time as a real input in your decision-making—not as an afterthought you check once a deal is already moving.

4.3 The Bigger Dollar Cap and What It Changes in Practice

Most tax breaks are like coupons: mildly satisfying, easy to misplace, rarely life-changing. QSBS is the odd one that can act more like a second exit—because at the scale startups can reach, the cap can be worth more than the difference between a "good" valuation and a "great" one.

That's why the post-2025 headline—raising the per-issuer exclusion cap for post-effective-date QSBS from $10 million to $15 million—lands with a thud in founder group chats. It sounds like a simple upgrade. In practice it changes three things that matter in the real world: how you model upside, how you structure ownership across taxpayers, and how much you care about documentation *before* anyone whispers the word "acquisition."

The temptation is to treat $15 million as a "problem solved" number. As in: "I'll never hit that; I don't need to track this carefully." Or the opposite: "I'll definitely hit that; I'll get $15 million excluded no matter what." Both instincts are wrong in predictable ways. The expanded cap is powerful, but it still sits inside the same architecture: it's per issuer, and it's per taxpayer, and it still competes with the alternative limitation—generally the greater of a flat dollar amount or 10× basis.

That last phrase, "10× basis," is the quiet force that keeps the cap from being a simple ceiling. Basis is your tax "starting point" in the shares—roughly what you paid (or were treated as paying). For a low-basis founder, the flat cap is usually the main event. For an angel who wrote a meaningful check, 10× basis can be the bigger number and the real driver. The post-2025 increase to $15 million changes the balance for many founders and early employees, and for some angels it's almost irrelevant because 10× basis already dwarfs the flat cap.

Why $5 million more can matter as much as a tax rate

A higher cap doesn't change the *rate* on taxable gain. It changes the *amount of gain that never sees a rate at all.* That distinction is the reason the cap can dominate.

Consider a founder with a classic profile: lots of shares, tiny basis. Suppose a block of post-2025 stock produces $20 million of gain at exit. Under the older $10 million cap, the "extra" $10 million would generally be taxable even if everything else qualified. Under the post-2025 $15 million cap, only $5 million is left exposed. At a 23.8% federal capital gains + net investment income tax rate, that extra $5 million of excluded gain is worth about $1.19 million in federal tax savings. That's not an abstract win. It's a second liquidity event that shows up as "not paid to the government."

And that's before state taxes enter the chat, before AMT considerations for earlier QSBS regimes, and before you consider that the cap is per taxpayer—which turns ownership structure into a lever rather than a trivia question.

A cap increase doesn't erase the need to track: it increases it

The expanded cap creates a new failure mode: owners assume the bigger number makes precision less important. The opposite is closer to the truth. When the upside is larger, the cost of a record-keeping mistake scales up too.

Two specific tracking problems show up repeatedly in diligence:

Blending issuances. If you own multiple blocks from the same issuer—some issued before July 4, 2025 and some after—the cap and exclusion rules may not be the same across those blocks. If you model "$15 million excluded" across everything without separating vintages, you've built a fantasy. The expanded cap is tied to post-effective-date stock; you still need to know which shares are in that bucket.

Forgetting prior exclusions. The cap is not a "per transaction" gift certificate. It's a limitation that can be affected by prior sales of the same issuer's QSBS. If you sold some shares in an earlier liquidity event and claimed QSBS exclusion then, you may have used up part of your per-issuer room as a taxpayer. The new $15 million number makes the room larger for post-2025 shares, but it doesn't make "used room" disappear.

In other words, documentation is not an administrative chore; it's the foundation for claiming the larger benefit without hesitation or hand-waving.

The per-issuer framework still governs everything

Founders sometimes hear "$15 million cap" and accidentally translate it into "$15 million total across my life." That's not how it works. The limitation applies in a per-issuer way. Each qualifying company has its own ceiling per taxpayer (subject to the statutory mechanics and alternative limitation). That's one reason angel portfolios can be particularly interesting: ten successful QSBS exits can potentially generate ten separate applications of the per-issuer limit, rather than one pooled cap.

But that per-issuer framing has teeth too. It means you can't "borrow" unused cap from one company to cover another, and you can't treat a complicated corporate history as a single issuer if it isn't. If your company merged, redomiciled, or spun out assets, you want a tax professional involved early—not because the idea is mystical, but because per-issuer limits interact with corporate events in ways that can surprise even sophisticated teams.

For most readers, the actionable takeaway is simpler: keep your records organized by issuer and by block. When the time comes, you want to answer two questions quickly:

- How much gain from *this issuer* have I already excluded in prior years?
- For *this block*, which limitation controls: the flat dollar cap or 10× basis?

Those questions sound technical, but they're really just bookkeeping plus a single multiplication problem.

Where the extra $5 million changes behavior

The cap increase doesn't change much for small wins. If your total gain from an issuer is $2 million, a $10 million cap versus a $15 million cap is trivia. The extra $5 million changes planning when outcomes are big enough that you would have hit the old ceiling.

That tends to show up in three practical situations.

1) The "big but not unicorn" exit

A $150 million exit can create wildly different outcomes for different shareholders. A founder with low basis might be capped under the old rules and only partially sheltered. Under the post-2025 $15 million cap, more of that founder's gain can be excluded—sometimes enough to change how they think about deal structure.

For example, when a buyer proposes a mix of cash and rollover equity, the founder isn't just comparing "taxed now versus taxed later." They're comparing "how much of the cash portion falls inside my exclusion room." A higher cap can make a cash-heavy deal more attractive because more of the cash can be paired with excluded gain—again, assuming other requirements are satisfied.

2) The late-stage employee with a meaningful common position

Employees sometimes end up with a surprisingly founder-like outcome: very low basis (exercise price), very high appreciation, meaningful total gain. Under a $10 million cap, an employee's "life-changing" win could still carry a large taxable tail. Under $15 million, that tail may shrink substantially, making the marginal value of waiting for a better tier (for post-2025 shares) or negotiating timing more tangible.

What changes in practice is the seriousness with which employees treat their own records. When the potential benefit is small, employees often trust the company portal and move on. When it's $15 million of potentially excluded gain, employees start acting like investors—and they should.

3) The founder who raised money at a high valuation and worries about being "too successful"

A higher cap doesn't fix eligibility problems, but it changes the payoff for solving them. If your company is borderline on qualification issues, it may be worth getting a formal internal analysis and cleaning up documentation because the reward is larger for post-2025 issuances. When the cap was lower, teams sometimes treated QSBS as "nice to have." With $15 million on the line per taxpayer per issuer, the calculus changes.

Flat cap versus 10× basis: who actually cares about which?

The alternative limitation—generally the greater of a flat dollar amount or 10× basis—creates two archetypes.

The low-basis holder. Founders and early employees often have minimal basis. For them, 10× basis might be $20,000 or $200,000. The flat dollar cap dominates. The move from $10 million to $15 million is the main improvement, because it expands the portion of gain that can be fully excluded.

The high-basis investor. An angel who invests $2 million has a 10× basis number of $20 million. That can exceed even the $15 million flat cap. In that case, the new cap may not be the binding constraint; the investor's own invested amount is what sets the limit. For these investors, the bigger story may be the tiered schedule (earlier partial exclusion for post-2025 stock) or simply ensuring the investment qualifies at all.

A compact example helps clarify which lever is doing the work. Assume post-2025 qualifying stock and a $30 million gain at exit:

Holder profile	*Basis*	*10× basis*	*Likely controlling limit*
Founder (very low basis)	$5,000	$50,000	Flat cap ($15M post-2025)
Employee (modest basis)	$150,000	$1,500,000	Flat cap ($15M post-2025)
Angel (meaningful check)	$2,000,000	$20,000,000	10× basis ($20M)

Table 4.3: The expanded $15M cap matters most for low-basis holders; larger-check investors may be governed by 10× basis.

Notice what this implies for planning conversations. A founder and an angel can be in the same deal, in the same company, with the same exit price, and yet the "cap story" is totally different. The founder cares deeply about the flat cap moving to $15 million. The angel may shrug because their 10× basis number is already higher.

That's why generic QSBS chatter is so often misleading. The right question isn't "What's the cap now?" It's "Which limitation controls for my blocks, and how close am I to it?"

The cap is per taxpayer: structure becomes a lever (and a responsibility)

The expanded $15 million cap applies per taxpayer, not per household in the casual sense of "we're married, it's all ours." That framing is the reason spouses, trusts, and other entities show up in QSBS conversations. Done thoughtfully and early, ownership structure can increase the amount of gain eligible for exclusion across multiple taxpayers. Done sloppily or at the last minute, it can create transfers that don't produce the intended tax result—or worse, create avoidable risk.

This is not a drafting guide, but one practical implication is worth stating plainly: if you might have an outcome that hits the cap, you want clean taxpayer-level tracking now. The bare minimum is to maintain separate ledgers for:

- who owns what blocks today,
- how each taxpayer acquired those blocks,
- basis per taxpayer per block,
- and any transfers that occurred along the way.

When you later ask an advisor, "How much of my gain can be excluded?" they can only answer after knowing *whose* gain it is. The expanded cap increases the upside of getting that right, but it also increases the penalty for assuming you can reconstruct ownership casually from a cap table screenshot.

Inflation indexing: a quiet feature with a timing implication

The law also brings inflation indexing mechanics into the picture, generally beginning for taxable years beginning after 2026. That's the kind of phrase that makes eyes glaze over—until you realize it means the dollar amounts aren't necessarily frozen forever.

Two practical ways to think about this without getting lost in statutory weeds:

- For near-term planning (an exit in the next year or two), assume the published dollar cap is the one you're working with unless your tax advisor tells you otherwise.
- For long-term planning (a 2030+ exit), don't treat $15 million as a permanent constant. The nominal cap may increase over time, which can slightly change how much room you expect to have—especially if you're modeling multiple future liquidity events.

This is also a reminder that QSBS isn't a one-time math problem. It's a living set of constraints that can evolve with both law changes and your own transaction history.

A "cap-first" modeling approach that actually helps during deal pressure

When acquisition conversations heat up, founders often model taxes backward: start with a purchase price, subtract rough tax, and hope the remainder is comforting. A cap increase invites a more surgical approach that can be done quickly if your block ledger is clean.

Here's a workable workflow for a first-pass model:

1. Break your shares into blocks by issuance date and taxpayer owner (as already organized).
2. For each block, estimate gain (expected proceeds allocated to that block minus basis).

3. For post-2025 qualifying blocks, compute the maximum potentially excludable gain under both limits: the flat $15 million and 10× basis.
4. Apply the relevant exclusion percentage based on the time milestone reached for that post-2025 block (50%/75%/100%).
5. For older blocks, apply the older regime rules.
6. Sum taxable gain and estimate tax.

This isn't meant to replace a CPA's work. It's meant to keep you from making bad decisions with good confidence. The expanded cap makes the wrong model more dangerous because the stakes are higher; it also makes a simple, well-organized model more valuable because you can spot which lever matters most: time, cap room, or basis.

Records that matter more now that the cap is bigger

When the cap was $10 million, some founders treated QSBS documentation like a nice-to-have add-on to the "real" work of building the company. With $15 million on the line for post-effective-date stock, the record list graduates from "tax nerd checklist" to "protect your net worth."

The most useful documents are not exotic:

- Stock purchase agreements / subscription documents for each issuance block
- Proof of payment (wires, canceled checks) tied to those issuances
- Exercise confirmations and payment records for employee-acquired shares
- Board consents and supporting issuance documentation (especially near key dates)

- A running log of any partial sales, transfers, or prior QSBS exclusions claimed for the issuer

That last item—the log of prior exclusions—matters because the per-issuer limitation is not a fresh $15 million every time you sell. It's a limitation that can be consumed. If you've done multiple liquidity events (secondary sales, recapitalizations, partial exits), a clean log can be the difference between a confident tax position and a panicked reconstruction.

The real change: the cap increase rewards owners who plan like professionals

The expanded $15 million cap is not merely a bigger number. It's a sharper incentive to treat QSBS like an asset that deserves management. It pushes founders and early employees to keep their own tax diary, not just trust the company's cap table. It pushes angels to maintain deal-by-deal folders rather than relying on memory. It pushes households to think in taxpayers, not vibes.

Most importantly, it changes the emotional stakes of timing and documentation. When the potential benefit is $200k, sloppiness is annoying. When the potential benefit is $1.2 million—or $3 million—sloppiness becomes a self-inflicted wound. The post-2025 cap doesn't eliminate the need for careful tracking. It makes careful tracking pay off more often, in larger amounts, with less room for improvisation.

4.4 The Higher Gross-Assets Threshold and Later-Issuance Planning

A startup can be "worth a billion dollars" on Twitter and still be a small business in the only way Section 1202 cares about. That sentence tends to make founders blink, because it clashes with how the startup world talks. In startup-land, valuation is the headline.

In QSBS-land, valuation is often just theater. The gatekeeper is the gross-assets test at the moment stock is issued—and after July 4, 2025, that gate got wider for post-effective-date stock: the corporate gross-assets ceiling increased from $50 million to $75 million (measured under the §1202 gross-assets test), while the $50 million ceiling continues to apply for stock issued/acquired on or before July 4, 2025.

This is one of those changes that sounds incremental until you run it through real behavior. A higher gross-assets threshold doesn't just help brand-new startups. It helps the messy middle: the company that's been alive long enough to have real assets, real cash, and real legal complexity—yet still young enough that new stock issuances are happening constantly. That includes later employee stock purchases, founder refresh equity, and new-money rounds. The bigger window can preserve QSBS potential for these later issuances, but only if you treat each issuance like a moment that deserves its own eligibility snapshot.

The easiest way to misunderstand the gross-assets threshold is to confuse it with valuation. Valuation is what investors pay for a slice of the company at a given moment. Gross assets, for QSBS purposes, are measured using tax concepts—cash plus adjusted tax basis of property—rather than fair market value. That mismatch is a frequent source of errors in later-stage planning, because it means a company can "look huge" while still having gross assets below the ceiling, and a company can "look modest" while quietly tripping the threshold because its balance sheet (as measured for tax) crossed the line.

A founder who has raised a splashy round will often assume the QSBS window is closed forever. That reflexive pessimism is understandable, and it is often wrong. The cash that came in with a financing is an asset, but whether it pushes you over a threshold depends on how much you already had and what the tax-basis balance sheet looked like immediately before and after the issuance. The nuance is not academic. It can decide whether an employee's later stock purchase is potentially QSBS or dead on arrival.

Gross assets: the number that doesn't show up on the pitch deck

Think of gross assets as the company's "tax-basis backpack" at issuance: what cash is in there, plus the adjusted tax basis of what the company owns. *Adjusted tax basis* is not what the asset would sell for on a good day; it's generally what the company paid for it (with adjustments over time). For startups, that often means cash dominates, because software companies don't have factories and land on the books. But as companies mature, you can have significant property, acquired teams, capitalized costs, or other items that make the tax-basis view diverge from a simple bank-balance view.

This is why the gross-assets ceiling is both generous and unforgiving. Generous, because it is not "market cap." Unforgiving, because it is a precise test at a precise moment, and it doesn't care about your narrative. A company can be extremely valuable because of product-market fit, network effects, or future cash flow—and still have relatively modest gross assets for §1202 purposes. Conversely, a company can be in a capital-intensive or acquisition-heavy phase and push gross assets up quickly even if the valuation isn't breathtaking.

The post-2025 increase to $75 million matters because it expands the range of companies that can truthfully say, "Later issuances might still qualify." It extends the runway for making new QSBS-eligible issuances without having to contort corporate strategy around a tax rule.

Eligibility is tested at issuance, not once-per-company

A persistent misconception is that QSBS status is a one-time corporate label: the company either "is QSBS" or "isn't." As you saw earlier in a different context, the reality is more granular. Eligibility is tested at issuance. That means later tranches deserve a fresh look.

This is where the raised threshold changes behavior. Under the old $50 million ceiling, many later-stage startups simply assumed they'd aged out. Under the $75 million ceiling for post-effective-date issuances, there's a new middle ground: a company might have crossed $50 million but still be below $75 million, meaning pre-July 4, 2025 issuances are constrained by the old ceiling, while post-July 4, 2025 issuances potentially still have room—again, depending on the company's gross assets at the time each block of stock is issued.

That creates a weird but practical outcome: two employees exercising in different months can end up with different QSBS potential, not because one was "early" in the cultural sense, but because one's issuance date fell on the safe side of an asset threshold and the other's didn't. The company's valuation may not have budged at all. The bank account might have.

The later-issuance moments that now matter a lot more

The raised ceiling mostly shows up in ordinary corporate life—moments that don't feel like tax events when you're living through them.

Employee purchases near a financing. The most common scenario looks like this: an employee is considering buying shares (through a stock purchase triggered by an exercise) and the company is about to close a big round. The employee's instinct is to wait—why rush, especially when the shares are illiquid? The QSBS instinct is to ask a sharper question: "Will the company's gross assets be under the ceiling at issuance if I do this now, and might they cross it after the financing cash lands?" Because the gross-assets test is measured at issuance, the timing of that purchase can matter. Under the $75 million ceiling, the "safe window" may be longer than it used to be, but it can still slam shut quickly around a major raise.

Founder refresh equity. Companies often do founder top-ups or refresh grants once the business is real and the original equity split no longer matches the work being done. That equity is issued later in the company's life, sometimes after multiple rounds. The raised threshold can keep those later founder issuances within QSBS reach longer than before. But it also means founders should stop assuming "my founder shares are all one thing." A founder who receives additional shares post-2025 needs to treat that issuance date as an event that deserves documentation of the company's gross assets at that time.

New-money investor checks after "seed." Angels and smaller funds sometimes invest well after the seed round—bridge rounds, extension rounds, small strategic financings. Under the old ceiling, these investors often assumed they were too late. Under the $75 million ceiling for post-effective-date stock, "late" is not a synonym for "non-qualifying." It's a prompt to do diligence: ask the company what its gross assets were at the issuance moment and how it measured them.

The phrase "later issuances" can sound like a niche corner case. In modern startups, later issuances are the norm. Companies continuously issue stock: to employees, to advisors, to investors, in connection with conversions, and sometimes in connection with acquisitions. The raised threshold simply increases the likelihood that these everyday issuances can still live inside the QSBS tent.

Why financing rounds are especially timing-sensitive

Financing is where the gross-assets test stops being theoretical and starts behaving like a trapdoor. In venture-backed companies, the biggest single jump in gross assets is often new cash. If the company closes a large round, the day before and the day after can be two different universes for the threshold.

One reason this is tricky is that people anchor on valuation rather than cash. A $400 million post-money valuation doesn't automatically mean the company has $400 million of assets. A company can raise $20 million at a high valuation and still have gross assets nowhere near $75 million. The financing that matters for the test is the one that moves cash and other assets.

The other reason it's tricky is sequencing. A stock issuance connected to a round is not merely affected by the round; it may be part of the same transaction that increases gross assets. If shares are issued as part of a closing that brings in cash, the "immediately after issuance" moment can be pivotal. This is not the kind of nuance a founder should freestyle. It is exactly the kind of nuance that should be captured in a company memo at the time of issuance, when the finance team can point to bank statements and closing documents rather than reconstructing them years later under diligence pressure.

The raised ceiling doesn't eliminate the sequencing risk. It just means more companies will find themselves in the interesting zone between $50 million and $75 million, where careful sequencing and documentation can preserve QSBS potential for post-2025 issuances.

A practical diligence routine for later-stage QSBS windows

When you're early enough, the gross-assets test is almost boring: the company has little cash and few assets. Later, it becomes a real diligence item. The raised threshold makes that diligence worthwhile more often.

A good routine has two parts: ask for the company's work, and preserve your own proof.

Ask for the company's QSBS position. Mature startups increasingly have an internal analysis—sometimes a formal memo, sometimes a set of calculations maintained by the CFO or outside tax advisors. Ask whether the company has a QSBS position memo or internal analysis, and whether it can share the high-level conclusion for your issuance date. You're not asking them to guarantee your personal tax outcome. You're asking whether the corporate-level gross-assets test was satisfied at issuance, and how they measured it.

Confirm what "gross assets" meant in their calculation. The key is to verify they're using the §1202 gross-assets test (tax concepts) rather than GAAP book value or some internal metric. The most common error is not fraud—it's using the wrong measuring stick because it's convenient.

Document the conclusion while the issuance is fresh. This can be as simple as saving the company's written response, plus whatever attachment or screenshot shows the calculation date and methodology. If you're investing meaningful money or exercising a meaningful block, consider asking for a brief written statement that the company believes it satisfied the gross-assets requirement at that issuance. Years later, in an acquisition diligence process, that contemporaneous documentation is worth more than a perfectly worded email you send yourself after the fact.

If you're on the company side—founder, CFO, or counsel—the discipline looks similar: create a short internal file at each meaningful issuance date that records gross assets under the §1202 framework. Treat it like you treat option pricing documentation: not fun, but potentially decisive.

The "too high valuation" myth and why it's sticky

It's worth confronting why the valuation myth persists. It persists because valuation is public and gross assets are private. Your valuation gets announced. Your bank balance doesn't. Your pitch deck shouts the former and whispers the latter. And because the startup world runs on signaling, founders internalize the idea that "big valuation" means "big company," therefore "no QSBS."

The tax code isn't impressed by your signaling. It wants the number that sits behind the curtain, measured the way the statute measures it.

The raised threshold to $75 million makes the myth more costly, because more later-stage companies can genuinely still qualify for post-2025 issuances. If you assume you're disqualified based on valuation and stop paying attention, you can miss an eligibility window that is very real. The tragedy isn't that you didn't optimize. It's that you didn't even check.

What to do when the company is close to the ceiling

When a company is near $75 million of gross assets, later issuances start to resemble a time-sensitive offer. That's not a reason to stampede into a purchase. It's a reason to slow down and ask smarter questions.

For employees, the key is coordinating with the company in a way that respects everyone's constraints. Employees shouldn't pressure finance teams for bespoke tax advice, but they can reasonably ask: "Is the company tracking gross assets for QSBS purposes, and do you believe we are under the threshold at the moment?" If the company can't answer, that's a signal about governance maturity—and a cue to be cautious with assumptions.

For founders, the key is to recognize that certain actions can unexpectedly push gross assets over the line: a big round closing, a sale of assets, a large cash infusion, or an acquisition that brings in property with meaningful tax basis. If you anticipate significant equity issuances around those events—refresh grants, employee purchases, investor shares—consider building a simple internal timeline that pairs those issuances with an updated gross-assets calculation. This isn't about gaming the system; it's about not sleepwalking past a threshold that was designed to be measured at issuance.

For investors, the key is diligence discipline. If you're investing after the company has matured, treat gross assets as a closing condition for your own comfort. You're already doing legal diligence and financial diligence. QSBS diligence belongs in that set if the expected upside makes the exclusion meaningful.

The raised threshold is an opportunity, not a guarantee

The $75 million ceiling for post-effective-date stock is a bigger window, not an automatic pass. Companies can still exceed it. Companies can still fail the test at issuance even if they passed it earlier. And because the test is evaluated at issuance, *later* can be worse than *earlier* in a very literal sense. The raised threshold simply means that "later" doesn't automatically mean "hopeless."

The most practical mindset shift is this: treat every significant later issuance as if it comes with a receipt you'll need to show someday. That receipt is not a glossy valuation chart. It's a contemporaneous record of gross assets under the tax-based measurement at the issuance moment.

When you keep that receipt—whether you're the company issuing shares or the individual acquiring them—you preserve the possibility that later stock can still qualify under the expanded rules. Without it, you might still have a good outcome, but you'll be trying to prove it in the worst possible setting: when a buyer's diligence team is impatient, your documents are scattered, and the stakes are no longer theoretical.

Chapter 5

Maximizing the Exclusion Through Smart Ownership and Equity Decisions

Most QSBS wins are not decided at the exit table. They are set in motion much earlier, when a founder signs a restricted stock agreement, an employee waits too long to exercise options, or an investor treats a SAFE like stock when it is not. This chapter shows readers where the real leverage lives: in timing, structure, and ownership decisions that seem small in the moment but can change the after-tax result by millions.

5.1 Founder Stock, Vesting, and 83(b) Timing

The most valuable QSBS decision is often made at the least glamorous moment in a startup's life: the day the equity paperwork gets signed, when the "company" is still a folder of docs and a cap table that fits on one screen. That's the moment when a founder can accidentally delay the start of their QSBS timeline, or—just as easily—start it running while the stock is still nearly worthless and the tax consequences are still tiny. Years later, at acquisition time, those early inches of paperwork can turn into miles of after-tax difference.

Founder equity commonly arrives as *restricted stock*. You receive actual shares up front, but the company has the right to repurchase unvested shares if you leave. Economically, you might think you "own" the full stake on day one. Tax-wise, the IRS sees something more conditional: you have stock, but it's subject to a substantial risk of forfeiture. That risk doesn't just control whether you get to keep the shares. It controls *when* income is recognized under Section 83, and that timing can quietly affect your basis and the practical story you'll tell later about how long you held your QSBS.

Vesting is usually described like a motivational device ("stay four years and you earn it"). For tax planning, vesting is a schedule that determines whether the IRS treats you as having received compensation over time. If you do nothing special, each vesting event can be treated like you just received that tranche of stock at its then-current value. In an early-stage company, that value might still be low. In a company that's working, that value tends to climb. The problem is not just paying tax—you may be paying *ordinary income* tax on the appreciation between your grant value and the value at vesting, even though nobody handed you cash to cover it.

An 83(b) election is the lever that changes that timing. It's not a magic loophole; it's a choice about *when* you want to recognize income on restricted stock: now (while it's cheap) or later (when it may be expensive). You are telling the IRS, "Treat me as though I received the stock today, even though it's subject to vesting." If you make that election properly and on time, you generally include in income the value of the stock at the time of the transfer (usually close to what you paid, for founder shares). After that, future appreciation is generally capital gain rather than compensation, and the story becomes much cleaner: one purchase, one basis, one long arc of ownership.

That "one long arc" matters because QSBS rewards clean timelines. You already know the headline: hold long enough and a lot of gain can be excluded. But there's a practical reality underneath that headline. When you're trying to claim an exclusion years later, the most uncomfortable questions are the ones that start with "exactly when..." Exactly when did you acquire the stock? Exactly when did the restrictions lapse? Exactly what was included in income, and when? Exactly what's your basis? The 83(b) election can make those answers crisp, and the IRS likes crisp.

There's another reason early 83(b) decisions punch above their weight: founders tend to have *embarrassingly low basis*. You might pay $0.0001 per share, or a few hundred dollars for millions of shares. That low basis is not a badge of honor; it's a *multiplier* for tax consequences. If your basis is close to zero and the company sells for real money, nearly every dollar is gain. If that gain is eligible for QSBS exclusion, low basis is wonderful. If you accidentally convert appreciation into compensation income because you skipped or botched 83(b), the same low basis becomes a trap door: a lot of your exit proceeds may be taxed at ordinary rates before QSBS even gets a chance to do its work.

The timing choice can be framed in one sentence: file 83(b) and you pay tax (if any) on today's value; skip it and you may pay tax on the company's future value as it vests. Founders often hear that and think, "If it's cheap today, why wouldn't I?" The real answer is that you are accelerating tax treatment before you know whether the company survives. If the company fails and your stock becomes worthless, an 83(b) election doesn't refund your time or your hope. Depending on the numbers, it also might not refund much tax. The bet you are making is that the company's upside is large enough that it's worth getting the clock started early and keeping future appreciation out of compensation income.

Most founder grants are structured so the upfront tax cost of an 83(b) election is tiny. If you paid fair market value for the shares, or close to it, the amount you include in income may be near zero. But "near zero" is not the same as "automatically zero," and that distinction matters. If your company's fair market value at grant is higher than what you paid—because you joined after a funding event, because an 409A exists, because the company has meaningful traction, or because the grant documents include a discount—you may have ordinary income even on day one. Plenty of people learn this only after they've mailed the election, or worse, after they've missed the deadline and are stuck recognizing income as the stock vests at higher values.

The deadline is the part that turns a sophisticated tax strategy into a footrace. The 83(b) election generally must be filed within 30 days of the transfer of the restricted stock. Not 30 days from board approval. Not 30 days from your first day of work. Not 30 days from the moment you finally read your equity agreement. Thirty days from the transfer. If you miss it, there's typically no "pretty please" extension. The IRS treats it like a door that locks.

That makes one seemingly boring detail urgent: figuring out what counts as the "transfer" date. In a typical founder stock purchase, the transfer is when you acquire the shares subject to restrictions—often the date you sign the stock purchase agreement (and the company accepts it), sometimes the date the company issues the shares, sometimes tied to payment. Good counsel will anchor this cleanly in the documents. Messy paperwork turns it into a guessing game, and guessing is not a great foundation for claiming millions of dollars of capital gain exclusion later.

A founder who wants QSBS to work at full strength should treat the first week of equity as an evidence-building exercise. Years later, you may need to prove: (1) what you acquired, (2) on what date, (3) what you paid, (4) what you included in income (if anything), and (5) that you actually filed the election. The mechanics of filing matter because the 83(b) election is not "a statement in your head." It's a formal election governed by regulations, and the IRS has been explicit that it can be made using a written statement or Form 15620. People who treat it like administrative trivia often end up with a tragic paper trail: an unsigned copy in a downloads folder, no proof of mailing, no acknowledgement, and no certainty that the election was ever valid.

The practical best practice is to build redundancy into the record. Prepare the election correctly. Send it to the right IRS Service Center (generally where you file your return). Use a mailing method that creates proof you can retrieve years later. Keep a complete copy, including what was sent and how it was sent. If your life is organized enough to keep a cap table screenshot, it's organized enough to keep proof of a high-stakes tax election.

The grant documents are where the bodies are buried—in the sense that they contain the terms that later determine how the tax story gets told. Three items deserve special attention:

First: the vesting and repurchase terms. Confirm whether the company has the right to repurchase unvested shares at cost (typical) or at fair market value (less typical). The economics are different, and the risk profile behind the 83(b) decision changes with it. Repurchase at cost means the downside is mostly opportunity cost; repurchase at fair market value can introduce more complicated outcomes.

Second: the purchase price and valuation context. For founders, the price is often nominal, but "nominal" should still be anchored in a defensible fair market value narrative. Even at the formation stage, the board should approve the issuance and price. Sloppy approvals can complicate the claim that the stock was properly issued and priced.

Third: the exact nature of what you're getting. "Restricted stock" and "restricted stock units" (RSUs) sound like siblings, but they behave very differently. Restricted stock is actual stock now, subject to repurchase. RSUs are a promise to deliver stock later. An 83(b) election generally applies to property you received that is subject to forfeiture—restricted stock. RSUs usually don't give you property to elect on in the first place. People sometimes assume "my equity vests, so I should file 83(b)." That's how you end up filing paperwork that doesn't match the instrument.

The cleanest QSBS setup for a founder often looks boring from the outside: purchase restricted stock early, file 83(b) within 30 days, keep copies, and go build the business. Yet there's a specific kind of founder chaos that tends to break this: the "we'll clean it up later" approach. A few common variants:

The handshake-to-paper lag. Founders start working in January, but don't sign purchase agreements until June. Equity is then "effective as of January" in spirit, but not necessarily in tax reality. If the stock wasn't actually transferred until June, the clock and the income timeline start in June. Backdating documents to match the story can create a different kind of problem—one that is far worse than starting the clock later.

The missing payment. A founder signs a stock purchase agreement but doesn't actually pay the purchase price (even if it's $50) until weeks later, or never. That seems harmless until someone asks whether a real transfer occurred and on what date. Pay the money. Get a receipt or keep a record. It's not about cash; it's about integrity of the transaction.

The 83(b) that "someone else" filed. Founders often assume the company's lawyer handled it. Sometimes they did; sometimes they prepared it and handed it to you; sometimes they reminded you and you forgot. The IRS cares about what was filed, not about what a lawyer intended.

The cap table mirage. A cap table entry is not the same thing as issued stock. If you end up in a dispute, or an acquirer's diligence team gets picky, you may need board consents, a stock purchase agreement, and proof of issuance. QSBS planning isn't only tax planning; it's documentation planning.

An underrated benefit of filing 83(b) early is psychological: it forces you to confront the reality that founder equity is not just a motivational sticker. It's a tax asset with rules. Once you start thinking that way, you tend to make better downstream decisions about exercises, secondary sales, and anything that can interfere with the QSBS narrative.

The "taxable value locked in" part is where founder stock becomes strangely elegant. Suppose you buy a big block of shares for a nominal price, and the fair market value at that time is similarly low. An 83(b) election generally locks in that low value as your compensation element (if any). Your basis is essentially what you paid plus what you included in income. Then the company grows. If the company later sells at a dramatically higher price, much of that appreciation may show up as capital gain rather than wages. QSBS doesn't exclude wages; it excludes eligible capital gain. The 83(b) election is often the move that keeps the upside in the right bucket.

There's also a subtle timing interaction with the expanded 2025 QSBS landscape. You don't need to memorize effective dates to appreciate the planning instinct: your exclusion percentage and limitations can depend on when the stock is acquired and how long it's held. A clean, early acquisition date gives you the broadest set of future options. A muddled acquisition timeline forces you into a narrower corridor, where you may be negotiating an exit date while also realizing your tax clock started later than you thought.

Founders sometimes worry that filing 83(b) "starts something" that can't be undone if they leave early. That's partially true: if you leave and the company repurchases unvested shares, the election doesn't rewind time. You may have included some amount in income, and then the shares are gone. In many founder scenarios, the included amount is trivial, so the financial downside is minimal. The real downside is emotional: it feels like betting on yourself and then watching the bet not pay out. But the tax system doesn't grade on feelings; it grades on dates, values, and paperwork.

The cases where an 83(b) election deserves a slower, more deliberate look tend to have one or more of these features:

The stock is not actually cheap. If the company already has meaningful value, the income inclusion can be large. If you can't pay the tax comfortably, you are taking on personal financial risk for a planning benefit that might never materialize.

There's a meaningful chance of forfeiture. If your situation is unstable—immigration risk, health risk, co-founder mismatch, or a role that might change—the odds of losing unvested shares are not theoretical. The election doesn't create the forfeiture risk, but it can create a tax bill you'll resent if forfeiture happens.

The terms are unusual. Nonstandard repurchase formulas, side letters, or messy IP assignment timing can make the "transfer" analysis more complicated. Complexity is not a reason to avoid 83(b); it's a reason to insist on clean counsel and clean execution.

An especially easy-to-miss trap sits at the intersection of vesting and "founder refresh" grants. It's common for a founder to receive an initial grant at formation and later receive additional restricted stock—either as a top-up, a retention grant, or a restructure after financing. Each grant is its own property transfer with its own 83(b) decision and deadline. Treating the new grant like it's part of the original can create a surprise: you may have one block of shares with a long history and another block where restrictions lapse later, income is recognized later, and the tax timeline is shorter. At exit, that can turn into a patchwork of tax treatments inside what you emotionally experience as "my founder stake."

From a QSBS-maximizing standpoint, patchwork is the enemy. Not because patchwork is disallowed, but because patchwork complicates proof and planning. Multiple blocks of stock can have different acquisition dates, different bases, and different outcomes. If you want the benefits of QSBS to arrive cleanly at exit, keep your equity story simple wherever you can: know which shares are which, and keep records that make the timeline obvious to someone who has never met you and is reading your documents under deadline pressure.

Here's a practical way to sanity-check your founder stock setup without turning your kitchen table into a tax department. You want to be able to answer, quickly and confidently:

- What is the *exact* date the restricted stock was transferred to you (the date that starts the 30-day 83(b) window)?
- What did you pay, and do you have proof of payment?

- What was the company's fair market value narrative at that time (even if it was "essentially zero"), and is there board documentation supporting the issuance?
- Did you file an 83(b) election (written statement or Form 15620), and do you have proof that it was sent on time?
- Do you have a complete copy of the signed stock purchase agreement, the restricted stock agreement, and the board consent?

That list is not busywork. It's the foundation of the claim you are trying to make later: "I acquired QSBS at original issuance, I held it for the required period, and my gain is eligible for exclusion." You can have the world's best exit and still lose tax benefits if you can't substantiate your timeline.

One more founder-specific nuance: vesting schedules are often paired with founder departures, and departures create repurchases. Repurchases can be emotionally messy and legally tense, but they also create tax artifacts: which shares were repurchased, at what price, on what date, and under what authority. Even if you never plan to leave, your future self will appreciate it if your documents make repurchase mechanics unmistakable. If a company repurchases stock, you want the transaction to be easy to trace later so your remaining holdings' history is not contaminated by ambiguity.

A final mindset shift helps keep this all from feeling like bureaucratic homework. Founder stock is one of the few assets you may ever buy for close to nothing that can later be sold for life-changing money. When an asset has that kind of skew—tiny cost, enormous upside—the tax system is never going to ignore it. The IRS will ask for dates and values the way a bank asks for signatures: not because it's suspicious, but because it's how the system functions. An 83(b) election, filed on time and supported by clean documents, is a way of telling a coherent story from day one. It doesn't guarantee QSBS success—

other requirements still matter—but it keeps you from losing the plot before the story even begins.

If you want one line to remember years from now, make it this: founder equity isn't just something you earn; it's something you *document*. The documentation is what turns an early, cheap grant into a clean basis, a clean timeline, and the best chance that your future gain stays in the category where QSBS can do its job.

5.2 Option Exercises, SAFEs, and Convertible Notes

Startup people have a natural instinct to date their ownership story from the moment they took the leap: the day they joined, the day they wired, the day they signed the note. It's a great narrative. It's also a lousy tax timestamp.

Section 1202 is obsessed with a narrower question: *When did you actually become a stockholder?* Not "economically exposed." Not "contractually entitled someday." Stockholder. That single detail is why smart, early employees sometimes discover they're late, and why early investors sometimes realize their "multi-year hold" is mostly a pre-stock waiting room.

A clean mental model helps: there's a long stretch in startup life where you have *upside without stock*. Options are upside without stock. SAFEs and convertible notes are upside without stock. Those instruments can be fantastic deals, but they usually don't start your QSBS timeline because they usually aren't stock yet. As we saw with the original issuance rule and the stock issuance moment, Section 1202 tends to care about the moment shares come into existence in your hands—not the moment you started rooting for the company.

That gap between "I'm in" and "I own stock" is where planning lives. And the planning isn't abstract; it shows up in emails you'll actually receive: an exercise window, a financing conversion, a tender offer, a surprise acquisition approach. The question is whether the dates on those emails line up with the holding period you need to claim the exclusion percentage you're aiming for under the post-2025 regime, or whether you're about to learn what it feels like to be 90 days short of a life-changing tax result.

Options: the grant date is a feel-good date, not a tax date

Employees love the option grant date because it's the first day the company told you "we mean it." It's also the day your cap table line item appears in Carta or in a spreadsheet that looks like Carta. It's emotionally real.

Tax ownership is more literal. Until you exercise, you generally have a right to buy shares later at a fixed price. That right can be valuable. It can be liquid in a tender offer. It can even be pledged in some edge cases. But it usually doesn't give you QSBS stock because it usually isn't stock. The practical consequence is blunt: the QSBS holding period generally begins at *exercise* (or, in some early-exercise structures, at the time you acquire the shares subject to vesting and make the relevant tax election). If you're sitting on unexercised options, you're usually not accruing QSBS time.

That leads to an awkward but useful thought experiment: if the company were acquired tomorrow and your options cashed out, what would you actually be selling? Often, you'd be selling the option (or receiving compensation-like treatment tied to the option spread), not selling a block of stock you've held for years. Many people first understand this only after a deal is announced and the buyer's payroll team starts asking questions.

The most common employee surprise is timing, not eligibility. Here's a concrete timeline that captures the trap:

- 2026: You receive an option grant at a seed-stage company.
- 2029: You finally exercise (maybe because you're leaving, maybe because the company is clearly working).

- 2031: The company is acquired.

From a career perspective, you were "early" for five years. From a QSBS perspective, your stock (if any) has been held since 2029, not 2026. If the rules you're relying on require a longer hold for the exclusion percentage you want, you've quietly shifted yourself into a smaller benefit—or none—without ever changing jobs, without ever selling, without ever doing anything that *felt* like a tax decision.

This is where the psychology of options collides with the algebra of Section 1202: the best tax outcomes often go to people who do the boring thing early, not the heroic thing later. Exercising earlier can start the clock earlier. Waiting can be rational—especially if the exercise cost and potential AMT exposure are meaningful—but it is never "neutral." Waiting is a choice with a timestamp.

There's a second, sneakier option issue: exercising in pieces can create multiple blocks of stock with multiple holding periods. Employees do this for sensible reasons: cash constraints, risk management, or uncertainty about staying. But from a QSBS standpoint, it means your eventual sale might include shares held long enough for one exclusion tier and shares held too briefly for that tier. You don't want to discover that on the eve of a liquidity event while your CPA is emailing you phrases like "tranche-by-tranche."

If you need one operational habit here, it's simple: treat every exercise as creating a new lot of stock with its own acquisition date and basis story. In public markets, brokerages do this automatically. In startup land, you are the brokerage.

Early exercise: the rare option move that changes the whole clock

Some option plans allow "early exercise," meaning you can exercise options before they vest, receiving restricted stock that vests over time. This is the option-world cousin of founder restricted stock. The reason it matters is that it can move the stock acquisition date much earlier—sometimes all the way back to your start date—if executed correctly and documented cleanly.

Early exercise is not available everywhere, and it's not free. You may be writing a check for shares you might ultimately forfeit if you leave before vesting. You may also need to consider the tax election mechanics (the same family of rules that make founder paperwork so consequential). Still, for employees who join very early and expect to stay, early exercise can be the difference between "I worked there for years" and "I owned stock for years."

The catch is that early exercise creates paperwork gravity. You'll have a stock purchase agreement, a vesting schedule, a right of repurchase, and often an election deadline. If any part is sloppy—unclear transfer date, missing board approval, missing proof of filing—your future QSBS story gets harder to defend. The point isn't that early exercise is risky; it's that it demands adult-level documentation in a world that often runs on Slack.

SAFEs: you may be early money and still be late stock

A SAFE is a brilliantly simple instrument for what it is: a contract designed to become equity later, usually at the next priced round. Investors love SAFEs because they're fast, founder-friendly, and flexible. But for QSBS purposes, that simplicity can lull people into a timing mistake: the date you sign a SAFE, and the date you wire funds, are usually not the date you acquire stock.

The QSBS timeline generally starts when the SAFE converts into shares and you actually receive stock. Until then, you typically have a contractual right that will *become* stock later if certain events occur. That right might be valuable, but it usually isn't the thing Section 1202 is written around.

Here's the classic angel timeline:

- 2026: You invest $100,000 via SAFE.

- 2028: The company raises a Series A; your SAFE converts into preferred stock.
- 2032: The company exits.

The dinner-party version of this story is "I invested in 2026 and held until 2032." The tax version is often "I acquired stock in 2028 and sold in 2032." That two-year gap is not trivia. It can be the gap between qualifying for a higher exclusion tier versus a lower tier under the expanded 2025 rules, or between being safely past a minimum threshold and being stuck negotiating timing with a buyer who doesn't care about your holding period.

This is also why two angels who invested on the same day can end up with different holding periods. If one invested via SAFE that converted in 2028 and another invested in priced equity in 2026, their "start dates" aren't the same even if their bank wires hit the company account within minutes of each other. Startup financing instruments create parallel universes of tax time.

SAFEs can also convert in multiple events. A company might do a small priced round, then a larger one. Or a SAFE might partially convert in a liquidity event and partially in a financing round, depending on the terms. Each conversion can create separate blocks of stock with different acquisition dates and different bases. If you're tracking your holdings as "the SAFE," you're already behind; by the time shares exist, you need to track them as specific issuances on specific dates.

Convertible notes: debt first, stock later, and the calendar doesn't care about your intent

Convertible notes add interest, maturity dates, and debt-like protections. They also add a common cognitive error: investors treat the note issue date as the "purchase date" of equity for QSBS purposes because it's the day they committed capital and signed paperwork.

Economically, that's fair. Legally and tax-wise, it's usually not the equity acquisition date.

Until conversion, a note is debt. You may have the right to convert into stock, and conversion may be likely, but "likely" doesn't start a holding period. The calendar starts when you actually receive stock.

Convertible notes create extra wrinkles because conversion itself can be a little math factory. Interest may convert too, potentially creating additional shares. Some notes convert automatically at a priced round; others convert at the investor's election; others can be repaid. If you're thinking about QSBS outcomes, the key is to separate three events that people love to blur together:

- You fund the company (note issuance).
- The note converts (stock issuance to you).
- You sell the stock (liquidity).

That separation is also why recordkeeping on convertibles can be surprisingly valuable. A note conversion can happen quietly in the middle of a financing round. You may receive a PDF confirming conversion terms, but not a crisp stock certificate. Years later, you may need to reconstruct the conversion date from board consents, closing binders, cap table snapshots, and emails. That reconstruction work is expensive and stressful at exactly the moment you want your tax position to be calm and clean.

The "late stock" problem shows up at the worst possible time

Nobody panics about holding periods when the company is struggling. People panic when the company is winning and time suddenly becomes scarce.

The most painful scenario is the surprise exit: a strategic buyer approaches, diligence moves fast, and the company wants to close in 60 to 90 days. If your stock acquisition date is recent—because you exercised late, or because your SAFE converted only recently—you might be staring at a finish line that arrives before your QSBS timeline does.

At that point, you have only a few levers, and none are perfect. You can ask whether the buyer will delay closing (rare). You can explore deal structures that defer recognition (sometimes possible, often complicated, and not always compatible with QSBS). Or you can accept a smaller exclusion tier and move on. The theme is unpleasantly consistent: the decisions that matter most are easiest to make long before the adrenaline hits.

There's also a quieter version of the same pain: employees who leave. Many option plans give you a short post-termination exercise window. If you don't exercise, your options expire. If you do exercise, you're starting the stock clock at the moment you leave—precisely when you have the least information about whether the company will succeed, and precisely when you may have competing cash needs.

That's not just a tax issue; it's a life issue. It's why employees who care about maximizing after-tax outcomes should treat their equity like an asset class, not like a lottery ticket tucked into an offer letter. Asset classes deserve calendars.

Lot management: partial exercises and multiple conversions create multiple tax outcomes

Startups rarely hand you one clean, homogeneous block of stock. They hand you a mosaic: some shares from an early exercise, some from later exercises, maybe a second grant, maybe an RSU settlement later, maybe stock from a SAFE conversion if you invested on the side. Each piece can have a separate acquisition date and a separate basis.

The tax return doesn't care that you mentally group it all as "my shares." If you sell everything in one transaction, you may still need to report it as multiple lots. Some lots may qualify for one QSBS tier and others for another. Some lots may have enough holding period; others may not. Some lots may have clean documentation; others may require archeology.

A practical way to avoid archeology is to build a personal "equity ledger" the same way you'd track a rental property: a dated record of acquisitions, costs, and supporting documents. You don't need a fancy system. You need a system you'll keep. Even a spreadsheet works if it's treated like a source of truth rather than a someday project.

The key fields are not complicated, but they need to be consistent. Here's a template that works for employees and investors alike:

Field	*What to record*	*Why it pays off later*
Instrument	Option / SAFE / Note / Stock	Prevents mixing contract rights with actual shares
Date signed / granted	Grant date or investment date	Useful context, but not the stock acquisition date
Stock acquisition date	Exercise date or conversion date (or restricted stock transfer date)	The date your QSBS timeline generally starts
Shares received	Exact share count issued to you	Needed to reconcile to the cap table and sale documents
Cost / basis inputs	Exercise price paid; cash invested; conversion amount; ordinary income recognized (if any)	Drives gain calculation and the 10× basis limitation analysis later
Documents saved	Exercise notice; wire confirmation; conversion notice; board consent excerpt; cap table snapshot	Evidence that survives staff turnover and platform changes
Lot ID	A simple label (e.g., "Exercise_2029_03_15")	Makes it possible to report multiple lots cleanly

The best time to create this ledger is not tax season. It's the week you exercise or convert, while the documents are fresh and the company can still easily answer questions. At exit, the company's legal team is busy; your questions will be competing with the buyer's diligence checklist, and the odds of getting a clean answer drop.

Practical timing choices: what you can control, and what you can't

Employees and investors don't control everything. You often can't control when a SAFE converts or when a note converts if it's automatic. You usually can't control when the company raises its next round. You definitely can't control when a buyer calls.

But you can control more than you think:

Employees can control exercises. You can model what it costs to exercise, what taxes might be triggered, and what timeline you're starting. Even if you decide to wait, you're waiting with eyes open. And if your plan allows early exercise, you can ask about it early—before you're trying to make a decision inside a 90-day post-termination window.

Investors can control instrument selection and conversion terms. If QSBS timing is a meaningful part of your thesis, you can factor "stock sooner" into how you invest. Sometimes that means pushing for priced equity instead of a SAFE. Sometimes it means negotiating conversion mechanics that reduce uncertainty. Not every founder will optimize for your holding period, and many shouldn't, but sophisticated investors at least understand the trade they're making.

Everyone can control documentation. Even if the timing isn't ideal, clean records turn an imperfect situation into a defensible one. Sloppy records turn it into a fight—sometimes with your own CPA, sometimes with a buyer's diligence team, sometimes with the IRS.

A final reality check: being "early" is not a tax category

Startup culture treats "early" like a moral achievement. Tax law treats "early" like a date field.

That can be annoying, but it's also empowering. If you know that the QSBS timeline generally begins at exercise or conversion for options and convertibles, you stop relying on vibes and start relying on events you can see, calendar, and document. You become the person who can answer the boring questions quickly: Which shares? Issued when? At what basis? With what supporting paperwork? Those boring questions are the ones that unlock the exciting outcome: keeping more of what you earned when the company finally wins.

5.3 Using the Per-Issuer Limits Strategically

The per-issuer limit is the part of QSBS that turns an "in theory" tax benefit into a hard, numeric ceiling. It's also the part that quietly rewards founders and angels who think about *ownership mechanics*—how stock is acquired, in what blocks, at what basis—while there's still time to influence the result.

The rule (as we saw) is not subtle: under §1202(b)(1), your excludable gain for a single company is generally capped at the *greater* of (i) a fixed statutory dollar amount or (ii) 10× your basis in the QSBS you sell that year, with the fixed-dollar room reduced by prior-year exclusions for the same issuer. That "greater of" is the whole game. It's two measuring cups sitting on the counter. Your job is to make sure you're pouring into the larger one.

The fixed-dollar cap gets most of the attention because it sounds like found money: "Exclude up to $10 million" (and for stock acquired after July 4, 2025 under Public Law 119–21, the headline number is larger). The 10× basis alternative sounds like a technical footnote until you're holding high-basis shares—late-stage purchases, larger exercises, priced rounds, real cash checks—when suddenly it becomes the only way your exclusion keeps pace with the size of your gain.

Basis, in plain English, is your tax "skin in the game"—generally what you paid for the shares (plus amounts included in income in some situations). Basis is not how much you *wish* you paid, not what the shares are worth now, and not what you could have sold them for in a tender offer. It's a number with receipts behind it. And because one of your two measuring cups is literally "10× basis," the receipts matter more than the vibes.

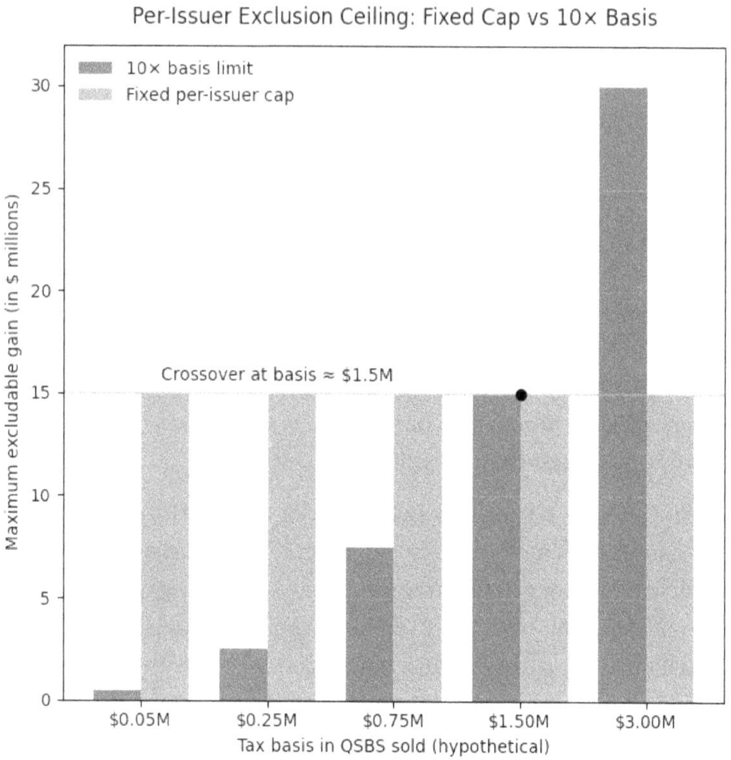

Two immediate takeaways fall out of the arithmetic.

First, low-basis stock makes the fixed cap the star. Founders with pennies of basis don't get a meaningful 10× basis number. A $5,000 basis becomes $50,000 of room under the 10× method—a rounding error in the kind of outcomes people associate with QSBS. In that world, the fixed-dollar cap is the oxygen tank.

Second, basis can flip the hierarchy. Once basis climbs, 10× basis starts to outrun the fixed cap. Around $1.5 million of basis (using a $15 million fixed cap), 10× basis is equal to the cap; above that, the basis method becomes the bigger measuring cup. That's why later-stage investors, employees doing expensive exercises, and anyone buying real stock for real money should not treat "the cap" as a single number. For them, the cap might be set by basis, not statute.

That raises a tactical question that's surprisingly powerful: *Which measuring cup is likely to govern my outcome?* You can answer it without guessing the exit value. You just need to know your basis and the regime that applies to your shares (including whether they were acquired before or after July 4, 2025). If your basis is tiny, you are almost certainly playing in the fixed-cap lane. If your basis is large, you might be in the 10× lane even if your gain is massive.

Why this "ceiling" becomes a lever

A ceiling sounds passive—something you bump into. In QSBS land, the ceiling is partly a reflection of earlier choices: how you acquired the shares, whether you bought stock for cash, whether a conversion or exercise created multiple lots, and whether you can document basis in a way that survives diligence and an IRS exam.

Start with founders, because they have the cleanest narrative. Founders often end up with very low basis, so the fixed cap drives. That can be wonderful—your basis being low is exactly why so much of your exit proceeds show up as gain that might be excluded. But it also means that for a single issuer, there's a point at which additional gain stops being excluded and starts being taxable. A founder who expects a large exit should treat the per-issuer cap as a real constraint, not a slogan.

Now look at employees and angels who enter through cash or cash-like routes. Stock purchased for cash generally carries basis equal to the purchase price. If you invested $2 million in a priced round and later sell those shares, you may have $2 million of basis, and your 10× basis ceiling could be $20 million—potentially more powerful than the fixed cap, depending on which cap applies to your shares. The same logic applies to employees who exercise large option positions at meaningful strike prices: exercise checks are not just pain; they are basis.

This is where the "lever" idea becomes tangible. Many equity decisions that are made for non-tax reasons—raising a round, exercising options, converting instruments—accidentally determine whether your QSBS benefit is limited by statute or by basis. If you know which lane you're in, you can model outcomes with more honesty and less superstition.

Scenario thinking beats exit guessing

The easiest way to misuse the per-issuer limits is to wait until an offer is on the table and then ask, "So how much of this is excluded?" At that point you're trying to do two hard things at once: reconstruct history and forecast consequences. It's much calmer to pre-compute a few ranges while there is no deadline and no buyer.

Three exit scenarios are usually enough to make the planning implications obvious:

- *Conservative outcome.* The company sells for a modest multiple. The fixed cap may never be reached, so the per-issuer limits are irrelevant. Great—your planning time can be spent on eligibility and documentation rather than maximizing a cap you won't hit.
- *Base case.* The company wins, but not in a way that breaks the laws of physics. This is where founders often realize the fixed cap is not an abstract number. A large founder position can hit the cap in outcomes that are "great" but not unicorn-level.
- *Breakout.* The company becomes a monster. Here, everyone hits a ceiling somewhere. Founders hit the fixed cap. High-basis investors often find the 10× basis lane gives them more shelter than they expected. People who assumed "QSBS means no tax" learn that QSBS is generous, not infinite.

This kind of modeling is not about predicting the future; it's about avoiding surprise. The per-issuer limits are one of the few QSBS constraints you can quantify early with minimal assumptions.

Basis discipline: the most under-loved part of QSBS optimization

"Basis discipline" sounds like a phrase that belongs in a tax department, which is exactly why it matters: nobody wants to do it, so the payoff is often real.

Here's what basis discipline looks like in the wild:

- *Cash purchases.* Keep the wires, subscription agreements, and closing docs. If you're an angel, don't rely on the portal's dashboard as your only record. Portals get acquired; logins break; PDFs vanish. Your basis evidence should be portable.
- *Exercises.* Keep the exercise notice, proof of payment, and the company's acknowledgement. If you exercised in multiple chunks, preserve the dates and amounts for each chunk. At exit, you may need to identify which lots were sold and whether any shares were held long enough for your target QSBS treatment.
- *Conversions.* For SAFEs and notes, preserve conversion notices, financing closing binders, and cap table snapshots showing the issuance. Conversion math is where memory becomes unreliable. A buyer's diligence team will ask for the conversion date and the number of shares issued. Your future self should be able to answer without "I think it was around the Series A."
- *Services and property contributions.* Basis can become complicated when stock is acquired in exchange for services or contributed property. The reason to bring this up is not to wander into drafting advice—it's to underline that not all "I got stock" stories produce the same basis, and the 10× method makes that basis outcome economically meaningful.

If you're allergic to paperwork, anchor to this: the per-issuer ceiling is calculated on your tax return, and your tax return is only as strong as the documents supporting its numbers. IRS Publication 550 describes the mechanics in consumer-friendly language, but the IRS doesn't accept "consumer-friendly" as evidence. It accepts records.

Diversification has a hidden tax feature: the per-issuer reset

A weirdly uplifting aspect of the per-issuer limit is that it resets by company. Put bluntly: five smaller wins across five issuers can produce more total excluded gain than one gigantic win in a single issuer, because each issuer carries its own limitation.

This doesn't mean you should invest for tax reasons. It does mean that diversification has an additional dimension: you are not only diversifying business risk, you are diversifying *per-issuer limitation risk.* Investors who build a portfolio of QSBS-eligible companies sometimes end up with a surprisingly large aggregate exclusion because each issuer gets its own measuring cups.

For founders, this shows up differently. Your wealth may be concentrated in one company, so diversification is harder. Still, founders often end up with side investments, advisor grants, or later-stage purchases in other startups. Those can matter. If a founder's main company exit blows past the per-issuer cap, gains from other QSBS issuers may still have their own cap room.

The "prior exclusions" detail that people forget until it hurts

The per-issuer fixed-dollar cap is reduced by prior-year exclusions for the same issuer. That sentence is easy to read quickly and ignore. It becomes painful for anyone who sells in stages.

Imagine a founder sells some shares in a tender offer and excludes gain under the fixed cap. Later, the company is acquired and the founder sells more shares. The cap doesn't reset just because a new calendar year arrived. You track what you already used for that issuer, and you subtract it from what remains.

This is why it's dangerous to treat QSBS as a one-time event. Liquidity often comes in episodes: secondaries, tender offers, partial redemptions, and then a final exit. Each episode changes the remaining room under the fixed cap for that issuer. If you don't track it, you can accidentally assume you have more shelter left than you do—or you can do the opposite and pay tax you didn't need to pay because nobody did the arithmetic carefully.

A simple habit prevents most of the pain: keep a one-page "QSBS cap ledger" per issuer that records (1) dates and amounts of QSBS gain excluded, (2) the method used (fixed cap versus 10× basis), and (3) what remains. It's boring, and it's exactly the kind of boring that makes an exit less stressful.

Pre- and post-July 4, 2025 stock: one company can give you two regimes

Public Law 119–21 draws a bright effective-date line: its QSBS expansion provisions apply to QSBS acquired after July 4, 2025. That creates a planning landscape that didn't really exist before: a single company can have multiple "vintages" of QSBS in the cap table.

Founders can end up with stock acquired early (pre-effective date) and additional stock acquired later (post-effective date): refresh grants, option exercises, secondary purchases, new-money investments, or conversion events that happen after the line. The point is not that one vintage is always better; it's that *you can't assume the same cap and holding-period framework applies to every share you own* simply because the issuer is the same.

Operationally, that means lot tracking is not only about exercise dates and conversion dates—it's also about which statutory regime governs the shares. If you have multiple blocks with different acquisition dates, you may have to compute exclusion outcomes lot-by-lot. That's manageable if you've treated your equity like an asset with records; it's miserable if you've treated it like an inspirational poster.

A grounded way to use the per-issuer limits before the exit clock starts

Here's a practical approach that avoids both paralysis and false precision:

1. *Compute your basis by lot.* Use actual payments and actual records. If you don't have records, get them while the company is still responsive.
2. *Decide which measuring cup is likely to bind.* If your basis is low, you're almost certainly in fixed-cap territory. If basis is high, 10× basis may be the governing limit.
3. *Run three outcome ranges.* You're not predicting the sale price; you're stress-testing whether the cap is even relevant and, if it is, which method dominates.
4. *Start a per-issuer cap ledger.* Especially if there's any chance of tender offers or staged liquidity.

The per-issuer limits are not a footnote to QSBS. They're the part that turns your equity story into a tax result with boundaries. Treat those boundaries like guardrails you can see ahead of time, and you'll make better decisions about exercises, purchases, and recordkeeping—decisions that often cost little in the moment and pay back massively when the number on the term sheet is finally real.

5.4 Passthrough Ownership, Trusts, Gifts, and Stacking

The per-issuer limits create a strange kind of pressure. They're generous enough to change lives, but finite enough that a big win can spill over the edge. Once you see that, a natural question shows up: *Can I spread this gain across more than one taxpayer so more of it fits under the ceilings?* That question leads straight into the most powerful—and most delicate—part of QSBS planning: who, exactly, is the taxpayer claiming the exclusion.

This is the point where startup equity stops being only a cap table story and becomes a family, entity, and paperwork story. The temptation is to treat ownership structure like a costume change you can do at the last minute. The law generally does not reward costume changes. It rewards real ownership held for real time, supported by real documents, with real economic consequences.

Pass-through ownership: the entity may hold the shares, but the benefit doesn't automatically "flow"

Partnerships and S corporations are called "pass-throughs" because income and gain generally pass through to the owners rather than being taxed at the entity level. That makes them an obvious place to look for QSBS leverage: if the entity holds the stock and later sells it, can the partners or shareholders claim the QSBS exclusion on their share of the gain?

Section 1202 says yes in concept, but it attaches strings that surprise newcomers. Under §1202(g), QSBS benefits are permitted through pass-through entities, but partner/shareholder eligibility is constrained—one key constraint being that you generally must be an owner at the time the pass-through acquired the QSBS and remain so. In other words, the entity's acquisition date is not a free-floating timestamp you can attach to whoever happens to be on the cap table later.

That rule is easy to underestimate because it clashes with how startup folks talk about funds and syndicates. A fund invests, then later admits a new limited partner. A startup SPV forms, then later someone asks to "get in". In normal business terms, that's routine. In QSBS terms, that late admission can mean the new owner doesn't get to claim *the entity's* QSBS holding history as if it were their own.

A practical implication: if you're investing through an SPV or a partnership and QSBS is part of the value proposition, the membership roster and timing are not clerical details. They are foundational. An "open" vehicle that takes new money after it already holds QSBS can create uneven outcomes among investors—some may be lined up for QSBS treatment and others may not, even though everyone writes checks into the same structure.

This also flips the normal instinct around flexibility. Many investors like vehicles that can be adjusted over time. QSBS tends to like vehicles that are settled early and then left alone, because eligibility is tied to who was actually there at the moment the pass-through acquired the stock.

The pass-through trap: joining the party after the stock is already in the room

The sharpest pass-through pitfall is painfully simple:

A partnership buys QSBS. Later, you buy into the partnership. You assume you "now own QSBS."

You may own an interest in an entity that owns QSBS. But §1202(g) is designed to prevent a kind of QSBS time-travel: buying into a partnership late and claiming an exclusion as though you personally acquired original-issue stock years earlier.

That doesn't mean late admission is always tax-disastrous, but it does mean you need to understand the rules before you treat "buying an LP interest" as interchangeable with "buying stock." This is where well-meaning investors get burned: they're careful about valuation, they negotiate fees, they read the SAFE, but they don't ask the one QSBS question that matters for the vehicle: *When did the entity acquire the stock, and when did I become an owner?*

If you're on the other side—running an SPV or managing a fund—the constraint becomes an ethical and disclosure issue. You can't market "QSBS eligible" without being clear that *who gets it* can depend on when they came in.

Transfers: tacking is the superpower, and §1202(h) is the rulebook

Stacking strategies often rely on transfers—moving QSBS from one taxpayer to another. Transfers raise a fear that sounds reasonable but is often wrong: "If I transfer stock, won't I restart the clock and lose eligibility?"

Section 1202 has special transfer rules that can preserve QSBS character in certain contexts. Under §1202(h), gifts and transfers at death are commonly discussed pathways that can preserve QSBS character and allow holding-period/basis tacking (subject to meeting statutory conditions). "Tacking" is the concept that the recipient can step into the transferor's holding history for certain purposes—so the stock doesn't become "new" just because it changed hands without a taxable sale.

This is one of the few areas of tax law where generosity and strictness coexist. The code gives you continuity for certain transfers, but it also expects you to respect the underlying realities: the transfer must be real, properly documented, and not a paper shuffle done after the outcome is already locked in.

The most common timing error is waiting too long. If a binding sale agreement is already signed, "gifting" QSBS can look less like a transfer of investment property and more like an assignment of proceeds—something the IRS has historically been skeptical of in various contexts. That's why sophisticated planning, if it's going to happen, happens before the deal is effectively inevitable, not after the champagne is chilled.

Gifts: the simplest stacking tool, and the easiest to misuse

Gifting QSBS to family members can be powerful because it can move future gain into separate taxpayers. The concept is straightforward: each taxpayer has their own per-issuer limitation, so multiple taxpayers can potentially shelter more gain than one taxpayer alone.

The execution, however, is where the difference between "smart" and "sloppy" shows up.

Smart looks like: a real gift, done early enough that the recipient truly bears the risk and reward of ownership, with proper gift documentation, updated ownership records, and a clear explanation of why the transfer happened when it did.

Sloppy looks like: a "gift" executed after a sale is already certain, with no meaningful risk transferred, no clean records, and an obvious tax-motivated fingerprint.

Gifts also force you to think beyond income tax. Shifting stock to another taxpayer can create gift and estate tax consequences, and the compliance burden can be real. If you've never filed a gift tax return, you don't want your first experience to be during an acquisition closing week.

Transfers at death: the planning you don't control, but your heirs will care about

Transfers at death are part of the §1202(h) story for a reason: they are among the cleanest examples of "new taxpayer, same stock history." The stock can pass to heirs, and the holding period can tack in ways the statute allows.

This is not a morbid planning pitch. It's a reminder that QSBS is not only a founder story; it's often a family wealth story. If the company is private and illiquid, estates can end up holding stock for a long time. If that stock is QSBS, heirs may inherit not only the upside but also the opportunity to claim an exclusion later—assuming the documentation is intact.

Which brings a practical point most founders ignore until it's too late: your heirs will not have your email archives. If the evidence that the stock was QSBS lives only in your brain, it's already endangered. Basic recordkeeping—issuance docs, acquisition dates, proof of payments/exercises, and any relevant elections—becomes a form of inheritance planning.

Trusts: stacking's sharpest tool (and why the IRS brought gloves)

Trusts are where stacking shifts from "clever" to "high stakes." The appeal is obvious: a trust can be a separate taxpayer. If it's a separate taxpayer, it may have its own per-issuer limitation. Multiply the taxpayers, multiply the caps.

But trusts are also where the tax law openly signals skepticism. The anti-abuse rule in 26 CFR §1.643(f)-1 allows the IRS to treat multiple trusts as a single trust when substantially the same grantor and primary beneficiaries exist and avoiding federal income tax is a principal purpose. That's the IRS saying, in regulatory form: "We see what you're trying to do."

There's also a more basic trust issue that trips up even sophisticated founders: separate-taxpayer status is the linchpin for stacking. Practitioner commentary often notes that irrevocable grantor trusts generally do not create an additional taxpayer for income tax (so they may not add a new §1202 cap), while non-grantor trusts may (facts dependent). As we saw in the grantor vs non-grantor framework, that distinction controls whether a trust actually creates an additional "measuring cup" or merely holds assets in a different wrapper while the same taxpayer remains on the hook for income tax.

This is why trust stacking is not a DIY strategy. It's not just about forms; it's about whether the trust is respected as its own taxpayer, whether the administration is real, whether the beneficiaries and grantor relationships are structured in a way that won't be aggregated under §1.643(f)-1, and whether the non-tax reasons for the trusts are credible and documented.

In other words: if your "plan" is to create five nearly identical trusts with the same grantor and the same primary beneficiaries, timed right before an exit, you should assume you are building an audit exhibit.

The tone of successful stacking: substance first, optimization second

The most persuasive stacking arrangements tend to share a vibe: they make sense even if QSBS didn't exist.

A founder might want to gift shares to adult children as part of broader family wealth planning. A founder might want non-grantor trusts for asset protection or multi-generational planning. An investor might hold QSBS through a partnership because that's how a fund operates, not because it's gaming Section 1202. Those non-tax motivations don't automatically bless the plan, but they help anchor it in reality.

Conversely, structures that exist only to mint extra caps tend to have brittle logic. Brittle logic cracks under scrutiny, under diligence, and sometimes under the simple passage of time when the parties involved can't remember why they did what they did.

The practical approach is to think of stacking like building a house in an earthquake zone. You can build bigger, but you can't build sloppy. The "engineering" is documentation, administration, and timing.

Timing: the moment you move shares matters more than the moment you think about moving shares

The single most common reason stacking plans fail is not that the law forbids them. It's that the transfer happens too late.

Once a sale becomes effectively locked—because there's a signed letter of intent with teeth, a binding purchase agreement, or a closing that is essentially inevitable—the stock begins to behave less like an investment asset and more like a right to proceeds. Transfers made after that point can be treated as assignments of income rather than true shifts of ownership risk. You don't need to memorize case law to respect the intuition: if the money is already "earned," the IRS is not excited to watch it move into a taxpayer with a fresh cap.

That's why serious planners treat transfers as something you do during calm periods, not during deal heat. Calm periods are when you can get valuations, update corporate records, file any needed returns, and make sure the recipient actually becomes the owner in every relevant system.

A stacking checklist that keeps you on the right side of "real"

This isn't legal advice; it's a realism filter. If you're considering pass-through, gifts, or trusts for QSBS outcomes, you want to be able to answer questions like these without squinting:

- *Who is the taxpayer claiming the exclusion?* Name the individual, trust, partnership, or S corporation that will report the gain.
- *Was that taxpayer an owner at the right time?* For pass-throughs, §1202(g) constraints matter: being an owner when the pass-through acquired the QSBS and remaining so is not optional.
- *Does the transfer preserve QSBS character and timeline?* For gifts and transfers at death, §1202(h) provides pathways that can preserve QSBS character and allow holding-period/basis tacking, but only if the statutory conditions are actually met.
- *Is the "new taxpayer" truly separate for income tax purposes?* Trust stacking rises or falls on separate-taxpayer status; grantor trust treatment can defeat the intended multiplication.
- *Would §1.643(f)-1 aggregation be a concern?* If multiple trusts have substantially the same grantor and primary beneficiaries and tax avoidance is a principal purpose, the IRS has an explicit tool to treat them as one.
- *Is there real administration?* Separate bank accounts, real trustee action, consistent records, and a paper trail that doesn't look

like it was assembled at the airport lounge on the way to signing.

Notice what's absent: cleverness for its own sake. Cleverness is not the goal. The goal is to end up with an ownership structure that is respected as real and that produces the tax result you modeled.

The most honest way to think about stacking

Stacking is neither "free money" nor "tax fraud." It's a spectrum of planning moves—some straightforward and widely used (gifts, estate transfers), some routine but constrained (§1202(g) pass-through rules), and some powerful enough that the IRS has built guardrails specifically to police them (multiple-trust aggregation under 26 CFR §1.643(f)-1).

If you want a guiding principle that holds up under stress, use this: make the ownership structure true on an economic and administrative level, early enough that the recipient genuinely owns the upside and the downside. Then treat QSBS benefits as what they are—an extra reward for getting the details right, not a prize you can claim by rearranging paperwork once the outcome is already certain.

Chapter 6

Exits, Reporting, and Audit-Ready Execution

The biggest QSBS mistake is thinking the hard part ends once the stock qualifies. In reality, the payoff depends on how the exit is structured, where you live, what gets reported, and whether your paper trail can survive scrutiny. This chapter shows readers how to move from "I think I qualify" to "I can prove it, report it, and keep the benefit."

6.1 How Different Exit Types Change the QSBS Outcome

In startup land, "exit" sounds like a single moment: you sign, you wire, you celebrate. Tax law hears something else entirely. It hears a very fussy question: *what exactly got sold, by whom, and when did the gain become taxable?* QSBS lives inside that question. When the answers line up, Section 1202 can feel almost unreal. When they don't, a headline purchase price can turn into a surprisingly ordinary tax bill.

A useful mental model: QSBS is happiest when *your* stock is sold in a straightforward "sale or exchange" and the gain shows up on *your* return as long-term capital gain at the right time. Every time a deal introduces an extra step—the company sells assets instead of stock, proceeds sit inside the company, consideration dribbles out over years, or your shares get cashed out in stages—you're no longer just doing QSBS math. You're doing deal-structure math.

Below are the exit paths you're most likely to see and the specific ways they change the QSBS outcome.

1) The clean stock sale: the QSBS "native habitat"

A classic stock sale is the easiest story to defend because the tax event happens where QSBS lives: at the shareholder level. You owned stock. You sold stock. You recognized capital gain. If the shares were QSBS and you meet the timing thresholds under the rules that apply to your lots, the exclusion applies to that gain (subject to the per-issuer limits and any prior use of those limits).

That simplicity matters in real life because it keeps you out of two common traps:

- *Trap #1: proceeds trapped at the company.* If the buyer pays the company (asset deal), you might not have a taxable event for a long time. QSBS is about excluding gain when *you* sell *your* stock. If nothing happens at your level, there's nothing to exclude yet.
- *Trap #2: cash now, tax later.* Some deal structures create taxable gain before you have the cash (or before you have the right kind of cash). A clean stock sale usually aligns recognition and liquidity in the same moment.

If you're lucky enough to be staring at a straight stock sale term sheet, the "QSBS work" shifts away from deal gymnastics and toward execution: identifying share lots, confirming the right rule set per lot (especially under the expanded 2025 framework), and making sure nothing about the closing mechanics accidentally turns a stock sale into something else.

2) Asset sale: when the company sells, but you don't

Asset deals are common because buyers often prefer them: they can cherry-pick what they want and often get a tax basis step-up in the acquired assets. The problem for QSBS is that the tax event occurs *inside* the corporation.

Here's the uncomfortable translation: an asset sale is the company selling its stuff. Any gain is recognized by the corporation. You, as a shareholder, typically recognize gain only when the company distributes the proceeds—most often as a dividend or in liquidation.

Why that changes the QSBS outcome:

- *Corporate-level tax can consume value before it reaches you.* QSBS excludes *your* capital gain on *your* stock; it does not erase tax the corporation owes on asset sale gain.
- *Distributions may not be capital gain.* Depending on how cash is distributed and the corporation's earnings and profits picture, you can be looking at dividend treatment rather than capital gain. QSBS doesn't apply to dividends.
- *Timing becomes slippery.* The company might sell assets today and then sit on cash for a year (or three) while it winds down, resolves liabilities, or negotiates earn-outs. Your taxable event might be delayed, and the character of income can vary.

Asset deals aren't "bad" in a moral sense. They're just a different animal. If QSBS is a major part of your expected net outcome, an asset sale is the moment to stop talking about purchase price and start talking about *waterfall math*: what taxes apply at the corporate level, what cash is left for distribution, what form those distributions take, and when shareholders actually recognize income.

Deal question that's worth asking early (because it's awkward late): *Is this transaction structured as a stock sale, an asset sale, or a hybrid election? If it's an asset sale, how are proceeds expected to be distributed and taxed at the shareholder level?*

3) Mergers and stock-for-stock deals: getting paid without "selling" (until you do)

A merger can look like a sale economically while feeling like a reorganization legally. Sometimes you receive cash (easy: that's a taxable event). Sometimes you receive the buyer's stock (harder: it might be tax-deferred). Sometimes you receive a mix ("boot"), which can partially trigger taxable gain.

From a QSBS perspective, two things matter more than the press release:

- *Did you actually recognize gain at closing?* If you received cash for your shares, you did. If you received only stock and the exchange qualifies as tax-deferred, you may not recognize gain at that time.
- *If gain is deferred, what happens later?* You may end up holding the acquirer's shares. QSBS doesn't magically attach itself to whatever stock you receive. The later sale of the acquirer's stock may have a completely different tax profile.

This is where founders get whiplash. They "exited," but their tax story is now: "I swapped into public company stock and I'll sell over time." That isn't necessarily bad. It can be great. But it changes the calendar: your taxable event may be spread out, and the tax rules may change with each sale.

Two practical wrinkles show up constantly:

Cash at close vs. cash later. A deal may pay a small amount now and more later (retention packages, escrow releases, milestone payments). Each component can have different tax character. QSBS can apply to eligible capital gain from stock dispositions; it generally doesn't apply to wage-like payments.

Multiple lots, one merger. If your cap table history includes multiple acquisitions (founder shares, early exercise shares, later purchases), the merger converts all of them in one legal event. Tax reporting still has to respect the lot-by-lot reality.

The "better question" here isn't "Is a merger good or bad for QSBS?" It's: *Which piece of what I'm receiving is actually consideration for my QSBS shares, and which piece is compensation, a continuation investment, or something else?* Your tax result will follow that answer, not the deal's nickname.

4) Tender offers and issuer buybacks: liquidity that can carry hidden QSBS risk

Tender offers and company-facilitated liquidity programs feel wonderfully civilized: no buyer diligence circus, no bank roadshow, just an offer to purchase a chunk of shares. For early employees, these are often the first time the equity feels like money.

QSBS, however, cares about redemption behavior in ways that surprise even seasoned operators. Certain redemptions and repurchases in connection with stock issuance can create QSBS eligibility problems. And tender offers are, at their core, a redemption-like event: the company (or a related party, depending on the structure) is buying stock back.

There are two separate QSBS concerns wrapped up in tender offers:

- *Your sale mechanics.* If you tender your shares, you're selling stock. That part can still be a "sale or exchange" that produces capital gain.
- *The company-level redemption backdrop.* Significant repurchases during certain windows around issuance can, in some cases, taint QSBS qualification for shares issued in that period. That risk is easy to miss because it's not about *your* tender; it's about the company's behavior and timing relative to issuances.

The practical implication is counterintuitive: a tender offer can be attractive for liquidity but still deserve a QSBS "safety check," especially if the company is simultaneously issuing new shares (new round financing, option exercises, founder refresh grants) or has been buying back stock as part of cleanup efforts.

This is also where your tax advisors will ask for things you may not have at hand: dates and amounts of repurchases, who sold, what percentage of outstanding stock was repurchased, and how that lines up against issuance dates. If a company wants to run a founder liquidity program and also wants the team's QSBS story to remain clean, those details should be treated like product requirements, not afterthoughts.

5) Secondary sales: partial exits, partial exclusions, and the per-issuer ceiling

Secondaries are the adult version of "take some chips off the table." They're common for founders, early employees, and angels: you sell a portion of your shares to a new investor, often years before an acquisition or IPO.

Secondaries can pair beautifully with QSBS. They can also create a weird emotional outcome: you sell a meaningful dollar amount of stock and still feel like you "wasted" some tax benefit. The reason is the per-issuer nature of the exclusion.

When you sell only part of your position, you are not "using QSBS." You are using *your per-issuer exclusion capacity* for that company. If the sale is large enough, you may hit your per-issuer limit earlier than you expected. Later, when the big exit arrives, the remaining gain can be only partially excluded because you already consumed the room.

This is why sophisticated sellers treat secondaries as both a liquidity event and a capacity-management problem:

- *Which lots are you selling?* If you have multiple lots with different acquisition dates and potentially different QSBS rule sets, lot selection is not just paperwork. It can change the exclusion percentage under the expanded tiered framework and can change which shares have reached the relevant thresholds.

- *How much exclusion capacity are you burning?* A secondary that feels "small" as a percentage of your shares can be "large" as a percentage of your remaining per-issuer cap.
- *Are you creating a mismatch between tax and cash?* If the buyer withholds, escrows, or staggers payments, you can recognize gain before you fully receive proceeds.

A clean way to pressure-test a secondary is to ask for two versions of the story: the *equity* story ("I sold X shares at Y price") and the *tax* story ("I disposed of these specific lots; here's the expected character of gain; here's the exclusion expected now; here's the remaining capacity for later"). If the second story is fuzzy, the first one is a trap disguised as liquidity.

6) IPOs and post-IPO selling: the exit that refuses to be one day

An IPO is often treated as the finish line. Tax-wise, it's more like a new phase of endurance training.

A few realities collide at once:

- *Going public is not a taxable event for you.* Listing shares doesn't automatically create gain.
- *Your taxable event is when you sell.* That might be months later after a lockup expires, or years later via planned sales.
- *Sales can be chopped into many small transactions.* That can be operationally messy: multiple sale dates, multiple prices, multiple lots, and sometimes multiple brokers.

QSBS can apply to post-IPO sales if the stock you're selling is still your QSBS shares and the eligibility and timing requirements are satisfied. The main twist is that IPOs often create *many* sales over time, which means your QSBS reporting becomes a recurring process rather than a one-time event.

Two issues pop up in the first wave of post-lockup selling:

Broker reporting rarely "gets" QSBS. The 1099-B you receive is typically built for ordinary stock sales. It may not track the right basis for equity compensation shares. It certainly won't label anything as QSBS. You can't outsource QSBS reporting to the brokerage statement and hope it lands correctly.

Lot selection becomes a real lever. When you're selling in tranches, you can often choose which lots to dispose of (subject to brokerage and identification rules). When your lots have distinct issuance dates, that selection affects whether a sale qualifies under the relevant timing tier and how much gain is eligible.

The headline risk in IPO land isn't that QSBS "doesn't work." It's that operational chaos turns a clean tax asset into a reporting mess. The fix is not exotic strategy. It's having your lot history clean enough that you can sell in slices without losing the thread.

7) Installment payments: getting paid over time changes when the gain shows up

Some acquisitions pay over time: a seller note, deferred consideration, or structured payouts. Economically, you may be "out" on day one and still be collecting checks for years.

Tax law generally doesn't care about your feelings. It cares when gain is recognized. Under installment reporting concepts, you may recognize gain as payments are received, not all at once (subject to various rules and exceptions).

Why that matters for QSBS:

- *The year-by-year exclusion math can change.* QSBS is often discussed as "exclude up to X." In installment reality, you're excluding eligible gain over multiple tax years. That can be helpful (spreads complexity) or painful (spreads uncertainty).

- *You may be living with future tax risk.* If future payments are contingent, disputable, or subject to offsets, the tax reporting becomes less intuitive. You need a defensible method, not a heroic spreadsheet.
- *State residency becomes more important.* If your gain is recognized over years, the state tax story can shift if you move, change residency, or split your time in ways that trigger competing claims.

Installments are one of those areas where QSBS optimism can morph into cash-flow stress if the deal doesn't deliver cash evenly. A buyer can be "paying" you while not actually funding your tax bill in the way you expected. Modeling the after-tax cash timing is not pessimism; it's basic self-respect.

8) Earn-outs: when the purchase price is a moving target

Earn-outs are the deal equivalent of "prove it." The buyer pays a base amount now and agrees to additional payments if the company hits performance targets. Earn-outs are common when buyer and seller disagree on valuation or when future revenue is uncertain.

Earn-outs complicate QSBS in three ways that matter in practice:

Character risk. Earn-out payments can be treated as additional sale consideration for stock (capital gain) or, depending on facts, recharacterized as compensation for services. Founders and key employees are the usual targets for that second interpretation, especially when earn-outs are tied to continued employment or performance metrics that look like a bonus plan. QSBS can't rescue compensation income.

Timing risk. The taxable recognition of earn-out consideration can be complex. You might have income in a year when the cash hasn't arrived (or when it arrives net of offsets). You might also be filing returns with estimates and later adjustments. That's not inherently fatal; it's just not the one-and-done QSBS fairy tale.

Documentation risk. Earn-outs live in the gray zone where a term sheet's casual language ("incentivize management") can collide with tax reporting. If the goal is capital gain treatment, the deal documents, board minutes, and payout mechanics should read like a purchase price adjustment, not like a retention plan wearing a disguise.

Earn-outs are not automatically bad. They are, however, the part of an acquisition where tax outcomes often "flip" based on small drafting choices. If you want QSBS treatment on earn-out dollars, the time to care is when the legal team is naming the buckets and describing the conditions.

9) Multi-stage exits: the quiet reality for founders and angels

Many liquidity stories are actually two or three stories stitched together: a pre-exit secondary, a tender offer, then a sale; or an acquisition with rollover equity, then a later sale of the rollover; or an IPO, then planned sales across several years.

The key QSBS implication of multi-stage exits is that you're not answering "Does QSBS apply?" once. You're answering a recurring set of questions each time you sell:

- Which shares (which lots) were disposed of in that tranche?
- Under which rule set and timing tier do those lots fall?
- How much per-issuer exclusion capacity remains after this tranche?
- Did this tranche involve anything that changes character (compensation, dividends, interest on notes)?

This is where disciplined shareholders quietly outperform chaotic ones. The chaotic version is reactive: each liquidity event is treated like an isolated transaction, and the QSBS analysis is rebuilt from memory under time pressure. The disciplined version is cumulative: each tranche updates a single running "QSBS ledger" that tracks lots, dates, basis, exclusion used, and exclusion remaining.

Deal questions that protect QSBS before the ink dries

QSBS outcomes are often decided before your CPA ever sees the closing binder. Not because CPAs aren't good at this, but because some tax outcomes are baked into deal structure and documentation. Here are questions that tend to surface real issues early, when there's still room to negotiate:

- *What exactly is being sold: shares or assets?* If assets, how will proceeds reach shareholders, on what timeline, and with what tax character?
- *Who is the buyer for secondary liquidity: the company, an investor, or a mix?* Company repurchases can raise separate QSBS sensitivity issues.
- *Is any portion of the payout conditioned on continued employment or services?* If yes, assume heightened risk that part of the deal is compensation, not sale consideration.
- *Is consideration paid over time (note, escrow, earn-out)?* If yes, model recognition timing and make sure you can report tranche-by-tranche cleanly.
- *Will you receive buyer stock (rollover equity) instead of all cash?* If yes, clarify whether the exchange is intended to be tax-deferred and what that means for later sales.
- *Are you selling enough in an early tranche to consume your per-issuer exclusion capacity?* If yes, make the trade-off explicit rather than accidental.

None of these questions are "tax nerd" questions. They're net-worth questions. The deal team may still choose the structure that's best for the company, the buyer, or the closing probability. The win is simply knowing, ahead of time, whether the liquidity you're about to celebrate is QSBS-friendly cashing out of stock—or a more complicated sequence where some of the economics leak into corporate tax, compensation income, delayed recognition, or capacity burn.

The most expensive QSBS mistake isn't failing a technical requirement by an inch. It's assuming that every kind of "exit" produces the same kind of gain. It doesn't. The label on the press release is marketing; the tax result follows the plumbing.

6.2 Rollover and Continuity Tools When Timing Is Imperfect

The worst QSBS conversations start with a sentence that sounds like good news: "Congrats—buyer wants to move fast." Speed is wonderful for closing probability and terrible for calendars. If you're sitting at year 3.5 or 4.2 and the deal is happening anyway, the tax question stops being "How do I maximize an exclusion?" and becomes "Can I keep the QSBS story alive long enough to earn it?"

Two tools show up in that scramble. One is explicit and statutory: §1045, a rollover rule that can *defer* gain if you sell QSBS before you hit the long-term milestone. The other is more structural: continuity through certain stock-for-stock transactions, recapitalizations, or reorganizations that may let QSBS attributes survive a corporate shape-shift. Both can work. Both can also fail in surprisingly mundane ways—missing a deadline, parking cash too long, or documenting a "continuity" story that doesn't match what actually happened.

The core idea: deferral buys you time; continuity preserves the thread

It's easy to confuse three distinct outcomes because they all sound like "I didn't pay tax yet":

- *Exclusion* (the QSBS prize): gain is permanently removed from taxable income, up to your limits, once the relevant criteria are satisfied.
- *Deferral* (the §1045 move): gain is not taxed *now* because you reinvest in replacement QSBS. The gain generally reappears later unless it becomes eligible for exclusion in a future sale.
- *Nonrecognition through exchange mechanics* (a continuity transaction): you may not recognize gain at the moment your shares are exchanged because tax rules treat the exchange as a continuation of the investment, not a cash-out.

They rhyme, but they are not interchangeable. §1045 is the "I had to sell too soon, but I can roll the proceeds into a new QSBS investment" rule. Continuity transactions are "I never really cashed out; I swapped into something that counts as a continuation" rules. Mixing them up is how people accidentally take a taxable event and then discover—late—that the cash is gone and the tax is real.

Section 1045 in plain English: the rollover option when the clock hasn't run

§1045 exists for a very human reason: small companies get acquired before early investors reach the long-term milestone. The statute offers a trade: if you reinvest the proceeds into new QSBS quickly enough, you can defer the gain from the early sale.

Two points that change behavior immediately:

1. *§1045 is deferral, not exclusion.* It's a time machine, not an eraser. The deferred gain is generally embedded into the replacement investment and comes back when you sell that replacement stock, unless you later qualify for exclusion on that future sale.
2. *You don't get to "think about it for a while."* The reinvestment window is tight, and cash sitting in a brokerage account while

you shop for your next deal is the most common way to lose the benefit.

That tight window is the practical center of gravity. You can be intellectually convinced §1045 is a good idea and still fail it because the new investment didn't close fast enough, the paperwork didn't line up, or you simply couldn't find a replacement company that met your risk tolerance.

The 60-day reality: why rollover planning starts before the term sheet is final

The rollover window is measured in days, not quarters. That creates an odd inversion: you may need to start sourcing replacement QSBS *before* you know whether your current company's deal will actually close.

If that sounds ridiculous, it's because it is—economically. But tax rules don't care that you'd prefer to wait for certainty. If you want §1045 to be available, you need a parallel track:

- Identify whether the stock being sold is eligible QSBS and whether you're within the §1045 timing range (sold "too soon" for the main exclusion).
- Pre-vet potential replacement opportunities that could close quickly if needed.
- Line up the operational plumbing (entity documents, subscription docs, wire instructions) so you can execute under time pressure.

The point isn't to rush into a bad investment for tax reasons. It's to avoid being forced into a binary choice at closing: pay tax now or panic-invest later.

Replacement QSBS has to qualify on its own

A rollover doesn't magically turn any startup investment into replacement QSBS. The replacement stock has to independently meet the QSBS requirements at issuance. That's where §1045 gets emotionally tricky: you're already dealing with the stress of a sale, and now you're also doing diligence on a new company's eligibility posture.

The investor mistake here is treating replacement QSBS diligence as a box-checking exercise. If the replacement stock fails QSBS eligibility, you haven't rolled anything—you've just bought regular startup stock and still owe tax on the original sale.

Practically, the replacement diligence resembles what you'd want anyway, with a QSBS overlay:

- Confirm the stock is acquired at original issuance (not a secondary purchase dressed up as something else).
- Confirm the issuer is a domestic C corporation and appears to meet the qualified small business tests at the time of issuance.
- Confirm the issuer's business activities aren't dominated by excluded service categories, and that its operations match its story.

Investors sometimes ask for a "QSBS letter." Some companies will provide a representation; many won't. The better posture is collecting the same facts you'd need to defend your own position: corporate status, capitalization, balance sheet snapshots around issuance, and a plain-language description of what the business actually does.

What §1045 does to basis and future gain: the "compressed spring" effect

A rollover doesn't eliminate gain; it often compresses it. Think of the deferred gain as being stored inside the replacement shares. When those shares are sold later, the old gain can pop out along with any new appreciation.

That can still be fantastic if the replacement shares eventually qualify for QSBS exclusion. But it changes how you should think about the future exit:

- Your "future gain" may be larger than the growth that happened in the replacement company alone.
- Your reporting file needs to preserve the rollover computation, because that embedded gain is not something you can reconstruct from a brokerage statement.

This is where people get tripped up in a later audit: the replacement stock sale looks like it generated an enormous gain relative to the cash invested, and the taxpayer can't explain the "why" because the §1045 math is missing. A rollover without documentation is like a passport with no photo—technically a document, practically useless.

Partial rollovers: the common case nobody models correctly

Not every early sale produces proceeds you can or should roll. Sometimes you need cash for taxes, debt, or life. Sometimes only part of the payout is eligible or practical to reinvest quickly.

§1045 can be used partially: you can roll some proceeds into replacement QSBS and recognize the rest as taxable gain. This flexibility is a feature, but it demands clean math and clean intent. If you're going to do it, decide explicitly:

- What dollar amount of gain are you deferring?
- What dollar amount are you recognizing now (and do you have cash reserved for that tax)?
- Which shares/lots does that map to, especially if your sale involved multiple lots with different acquisition dates?

A rollover decision made "in aggregate" can collide with lot-level reporting later. Treat the rollover as a designed allocation, not a vibe.

Rollover meets reality: earn-outs, escrows, and delayed payments

Not all "sale proceeds" arrive on day one. Deals often include escrows for indemnities, holdbacks, or contingent payments that resolve later. That creates a timing puzzle: §1045 wants reinvestment quickly, but you may not receive all cash quickly.

This is where the legal details start driving the tax result. Depending on how the deal is structured, you might:

- Receive cash now and later (easier to think about).
- Have proceeds withheld in escrow but treated as received for tax purposes (harder).
- Have contingent rights that are valued and taxed upfront (hardest).

If you're contemplating §1045, you want clarity on what counts as proceeds received in the relevant window and what doesn't. That's not a DIY corner. It's a "bring your tax person into the deal calls" corner.

The partnership twist: SPVs and angel groups can't wing it

Angels often invest through SPVs or other entities taxed as partnerships. That structure changes the operational question from "Can *I* elect a rollover?" to "Who makes the election, and what flows through to whom?"

Partnership mechanics are their own universe. The key practical point: the ability to make a §1045 election and the information needed to support it have to be coordinated between the entity and the underlying partners. If an SPV sells QSBS and wants rollover treatment, the timeline is still brutal, but now it's brutal for a group.

Common failure modes in group structures:

- Investors don't find out about the sale in time to decide whether they want to participate in a rollover strategy.
- The entity can't move quickly enough to make a replacement investment because it needs partner consents or fresh documents.
- Partners receive incomplete information (basis, allocation, dates) and can't support consistent reporting.

The solution is boring but effective: pre-negotiate the "what happens in a sale" rules in the SPV documents, including how elections will be handled and what notices partners receive. The tax benefit doesn't care that the SPV manager was busy; it cares that the reinvestment occurred on time and can be substantiated.

Continuity transactions: when you never touch cash, and the investment morphs

Now for the other category: deals where you don't sell for cash, at least not entirely. Instead, you exchange your shares for other equity—sometimes in the buyer, sometimes in a new holding company formed in a reorganization, sometimes through a recapitalization that changes the class of your stock.

These transactions can preserve QSBS attributes in certain circumstances, but they are not automatic wins. The phrase "stock-for-stock" can hide very different tax outcomes:

- A true nonrecognition exchange may defer recognition of gain entirely at the time of the deal.
- A mixed consideration deal (some stock, some cash) may trigger gain on the cash portion.

- A transaction that looks like an exchange might actually be treated as a sale followed by a reinvestment, depending on how it's documented and executed.

Continuity transactions are where terminology becomes dangerous. A banker may call something "rollover equity" meaning, "you're taking some of your consideration in the buyer's stock." That is not the same as a §1045 rollover. It might be part of a reorganization with nonrecognition treatment, or it might be a taxable sale with a reinvestment. Similar English words; wildly different tax consequences.

The practical question in continuity deals: what is the tax event, if any?

When your shares are swapped for other shares, the key is pinpointing whether the exchange is treated as taxable. If it's non-taxable, QSBS exclusion isn't something you "claim" that year because there's no recognized gain to exclude. Instead, you're preserving the investment thread into new shares.

That sounds appealing, but it shifts your risk:

- Your eventual taxable event is postponed, which can be great, but it also means you now need to track the inherited attributes into the new security.
- The new security may not be the same kind of thing economically or legally, and future sales might not be as simple.

This is where founders get surprised after a "mostly stock" acquisition: the tax story isn't finished at closing. It's now a multi-year reporting exercise until the received shares are sold.

Recapitalizations and cleanups: continuity can be lost in the paperwork

Private companies recap all the time: converting SAFEs, exchanging preferred for common, reorganizing into a new holding company, splitting shares, or cleaning up small holders. Many of these moves are benign for QSBS, but "benign" is not the same as "unimportant."

Continuity is fragile when the paperwork is sloppy. A recap that was intended as a tax-free exchange can be undermined by documentation that reads like a purchase and sale. Or the company can unintentionally create a redemption issue as part of a cleanup, as we saw earlier with repurchases being a quiet QSBS killer.

If you're a shareholder and the company is doing a complex recap, the right posture is politely paranoid:

- Ask what the company believes the tax treatment is and whether counsel has documented that treatment.
- Save the documents that establish the exchange mechanics, not just the cap table output.
- Make sure your own records show a continuous chain from original issuance to whatever you now hold.

The emotional trap here is assuming the company's lawyers will maintain your personal tax file for you. They won't. They're optimizing for corporate outcomes and closing the transaction. Your future audit defense is your job.

Choosing between §1045 and continuity: they solve different problems

Sometimes you truly have a choice; often you don't.

If you are receiving cash for your shares and recognizing gain, §1045 is the relevant "second chance" tool—*if* you can and want to reinvest quickly in replacement QSBS.

If you are receiving only stock in a qualifying exchange and not recognizing gain, §1045 may be irrelevant because there is no recognized gain to roll. Your focus shifts to tracking what you received, why it was nonrecognition, and how the attributes carry into the new shares.

A common confusion happens when a deal includes both: some cash out, some rollover equity. Now you may have both recognized gain (cash portion) and deferred gain (stock portion). In that case, you're juggling two separate concepts:

- continuity/nonrecognition for the exchanged portion, and
- possible §1045 deferral on the recognized gain portion (if the timing and reinvestment requirements are satisfied).

That's doable. It's also a perfect recipe for messy reporting if nobody is tracking which component is which.

A founder-at-year-3.5 example: the "fast close" dilemma

Imagine a founder with QSBS shares acquired at formation. At year 3.5, a buyer offers a strong price with a tight closing schedule. The founder's dream is QSBS exclusion under the longer-term rule set, but the deal won't wait.

In that scenario, the most useful reframing is blunt: *you're not choosing between "QSBS" and "no QSBS." You're choosing between "recognize gain now" and "try to defer gain into another QSBS path."*

If the founder takes cash and recognizes gain now, that gain is taxed under normal rules. If the founder wants a shot at eventual exclusion, §1045 offers a possible bridge: sell now, reinvest quickly into replacement QSBS, and hope that replacement investment survives long enough—and performs well enough—to be worth the trouble.

That's not a tax-only choice. It's an investment choice under time pressure. The correct answer can easily be "pay the tax," especially if the founder doesn't want concentrated risk in a new early-stage company or doesn't have a vetted pipeline of deals.

The win is deciding with eyes open and not discovering §1045 after the reinvestment window has already expired.

An angel-through-SPV example: coordination is the whole game

Now picture an angel who invested through an SPV. The SPV's portfolio company is acquired early, producing a gain allocation to the members. One investor wants to pursue §1045. Another wants cash. A third doesn't respond.

That's where rollover dreams die—not because the tax law is harsh, but because groups move slowly. If the SPV documents don't specify how these elections and reinvestments are handled, you can end up with the worst of all worlds: a theoretical tax benefit that no one can execute within the window.

If you invest through entities regularly and QSBS is a meaningful part of your expected return, the most valuable "tax planning" may happen before any sale exists: ensure the governing documents address notice, timelines, authority to reinvest, and how investors can opt in or opt out of rollover strategies.

A practical, non-heroic readiness checklist

When timing is uncertain, heroics are the enemy. What works is a small set of operational habits:

- Maintain a running list of your QSBS lots, their acquisition dates, and the evidence that supports original issuance and eligibility.
- If an early sale is plausible, keep a short list of potential replacement investments (or managers/funds) that could close quickly.

- For any deal with earn-outs, escrows, or mixed consideration, insist on clarity about what is treated as purchase price for stock and what is treated as compensation or interest-like economics.
- If you hold through an SPV/partnership, make sure you know who has authority to act, and what information you will receive in time to report consistently.

None of that guarantees §1045 will make sense, or that a continuity transaction will preserve what you hope it preserves. It does something more valuable: it keeps you from being cornered by the calendar.

Timing imperfections are normal in startups. The tax code's answer is not "too bad." It's a set of narrow bridges—§1045 deferral and certain continuity pathways—that can carry the QSBS story forward. They're sturdy enough to walk across, but only if you're already at the bridge when the deal closes.

6.3 State Taxes and the Reality of Net After-Tax Proceeds

A QSBS win can be emotionally weird. You run the numbers, see a giant federal exclusion, and your brain files it under "done." Then your CPA asks one quiet follow-up question: *"What state are you paying tax to?"* Suddenly you're back in the arena.

State tax is where QSBS goes from a great headline to a real cash outcome. The federal benefit is statutory and federal; it does not automatically determine state tax treatment—state conformity must be checked separately for net proceeds planning. That single sentence explains why two founders can sell the same company for the same gain, claim the same federal exclusion, and still walk away with dramatically different checks.

The most brutal version is also the most common: you planned your life around the federal result and only later discover the state result is basically "nice try."

The QSBS mirage: "excluded federally" can still mean "taxed normally" at the state level

The cleanest way to understand the surprise is to strip QSBS of its mystique. Federally, QSBS reduces taxable capital gain under IRC §1202 (and §1045 can defer gain in certain cases). States get to decide what they do with that federal story.

Some states conform closely to the Internal Revenue Code. Some conform partially. Some pick and choose. Some freeze their conformity to an older version of federal law. And some flat-out decouple from QSBS.

California is the poster child because the result is so stark: California primary-source guidance states California does not conform to the QSBS deferral and exclusion provisions under IRC §1045 and §1202—meaning QSBS gains that are excluded federally may be fully taxed by California.

That isn't a small technicality. It changes lifestyle math.

Imagine a founder with a $10M gain that qualifies for a full federal QSBS exclusion. Federal tax on that gain could be zero. California can still tax the gain as if QSBS doesn't exist. Same sale. Same stock. Same taxpayer. Two governments, two answers.

The point isn't to pick on California. The point is to treat state tax as an independent system that just happens to borrow pieces of the federal system when it wants to.

A durable framework: four questions that cut through the fog

A 50-state chart is tempting and often useless. What lasts longer is a repeatable framework you can apply to your own facts. When a liquidity event is coming, these are the four questions that drive the state result:

1. *Where are you a resident for tax purposes at the time the gain is recognized?*
2. *Does that state conform to IRC §1202 (and §1045, if relevant)?*
3. *If you changed states recently, how does the state treat part-year residency, domicile, and statutory residency?*
4. *Is any state asserting the gain is sourced to it anyway (even if you're a nonresident)?*

You can get every QSBS eligibility detail right and still lose the after-tax battle if you never answer those questions until after closing.

Conformity isn't binary: rolling vs. static conformity is the hidden lever

State conformity sounds like a yes/no switch. In practice, it's more like software versioning.

State outcomes depend on whether and how a state conforms to the IRC (rolling vs static conformity is a key explanatory framework for why federal changes may or may not flow through). In plain language:

- A *rolling conformity* state updates automatically as federal tax law changes (at least in theory).
- A *static conformity* state conforms to the IRC as of a specific date—like "federal tax law as it existed on January 1, 20XX." Federal improvements after that date may not show up on the state return unless the legislature updates the conformity date.

Why this matters under the expanded 2025 rules: a founder can do everything right federally and still discover that their state is effectively living in an older QSBS universe. If you're modeling after-tax outcomes based on federal expansions, static conformity can quietly erase that model at the state level.

Practitioner memos can be used to highlight that state nonconformity is a common real-world surprise and should be modeled early in an exit process. "Early" here means before you commit to a deal structure, before you decide how much stock to sell in a secondary, and before you decide whether moving states is worth the upheaval.

Residency: the most expensive "soft" concept in the tax code

If conformity is the law, residency is the battlefield. Residency determines which state gets the first claim on your capital gains. And states take residency personally.

Two words drive most high-stakes state fights:

- *Domicile*—your true home—the place you intend to return to and stay.
- *Statutory residency*—a rules-based residency test that can apply even if you claim your "real" home is elsewhere (often tied to days spent and maintaining a place to live).

Founders underestimate how invasive this becomes because they think in startup terms: "I moved. I updated my address. I'm done." States think in evidence: Where is your family? Where is your primary home? Where do you vote? Where are your doctors? Where are your cars registered? Where are your prized personal items? Where do you spend time?

If the sale is large enough, your calendar becomes a legal document.

A late move—six months before signing, or worse, after an LOI—can still be real, but it's harder to defend. Not because moving is illegal; because moving *for tax reasons* is so common that states have built a whole apparatus to distinguish "changed my life" from "changed my mailing address."

The only honest rule: if you want a move to matter, it has to look like a move in every part of your life, not just on the tax return.

Sourcing: the nonresident tax bill that shows up uninvited

Many people assume capital gains are taxed only by the state where you live. Often that's true for stock sales. But "often" isn't good enough when seven figures are on the line.

Some states may try to tax certain gains of nonresidents based on sourcing rules—rules that ask whether the income is connected to the state in some way. The details are intensely state-specific, and this is exactly the point where generic QSBS advice becomes dangerous. Still, two practical implications are worth carrying around:

- You can be a nonresident and still receive a state tax notice if the state believes it has a sourcing hook.
- Complex exits create more hooks: installment payments recognized across years, earn-outs tied to continued work in a state, or allocations through pass-through entities operating in multiple states.

This is one reason multi-stage exits are so annoying: the "state picture" can change across time. If gain is recognized over multiple tax years, your residency and sourcing facts can shift across those years, which can shift the state tax result.

The planning trap: treating state tax as a post-close spreadsheet exercise

State planning is often done backward. The deal closes, the wire hits, and then someone asks, "Should we have done anything about state tax?" That's like asking whether you should have worn a parachute after you land.

If there's one mindset shift that reliably improves outcomes, it's this: state tax planning is less about cleverness and more about *timing and consistency*. When it works, it's because the facts were put in place early enough to be real.

This is also where founders get tempted by shiny tactics—renting an apartment, changing a driver's license, spending a handful of days elsewhere. Superficial moves can backfire because they create contradictory evidence. A state auditor doesn't need to prove you never left; they need to show you never truly arrived somewhere else.

Secondary sales and partial liquidity: state tax can change the "best tranche" to sell

Earlier we talked about multi-stage exits and how they interact with per-issuer limits. State tax adds another dimension: *which tranche you sell, and when, can change which state gets to tax it.*

Consider a founder who expects a large federal QSBS exclusion and is thinking about selling shares in a pre-exit secondary. If that founder later moves (for real reasons, or tax reasons, or both), the state tax result might make the secondary either:

- a smart early liquidity move (if it occurs while resident in a conforming state), or
- an unexpectedly expensive event (if it occurs while resident in a nonconforming state), even if the federal QSBS outcome is excellent.

That's why it's dangerous to evaluate secondaries purely as "risk reduction." They also allocate gain across time, which can allocate gain across states.

The California example, properly used: not as fear, but as math

California's nonconformity is useful because it forces clarity. When someone says "I'm excluding it under QSBS," the correct follow-up is: *"Federally, yes. What about your state?"*

Even if you never set foot in California, treat that example as a mental unit test. If your model doesn't explicitly include state tax assumptions, your model is incomplete.

A robust after-tax model should show:

- Federal tax on the eligible gain (often reduced by QSBS).
- State tax on the same gain under two scenarios: state conforms versus state does not conform.
- The net cash retained under each scenario.

If the net swing is large, state planning becomes a first-order issue, not a footnote.

When a move might matter—and when it probably won't

A move can be powerful, but it has a countdown clock. The closer you get to a signed deal, the more skeptical a state may be, and the more evidence you need.

Scenarios where timing tends to be unfavorable:

- You move after an LOI is signed and the sale price is largely locked.
- You keep your primary home, your family, and your daily life in the old state and claim the new state based on paperwork.
- You recognize gain across multiple years (installments, earn-outs), and you move midstream without clear documentation of residency changes by year.

Scenarios where a move has a better chance of being respected:

- You relocate well before a deal is imminent and your life actually re-centers.

- You maintain consistent records: day counts, leases or home purchase, voter registration, driver's license, professional ties, and the non-glamorous trail of everyday living.

None of this is legal advice, and it's not meant to scare you into paralysis. It's meant to keep you from confusing "possible" with "easy."

Multi-state lives: the new normal for founders creates new audit narratives

Modern founders are mobile by default: a place in Austin, investors in New York, a team in SF, time in Miami, parents somewhere else. That lifestyle is fantastic. It also creates overlapping state narratives.

If you live a multi-state life, the "state tax file" becomes part of being audit-ready:

- Keep a defensible day-count record (not reconstructed from memory).
- Keep evidence of where you actually lived and worked in the year the gain is recognized.
- Coordinate the story across documents: brokerage addresses, employer payroll records, driver's license, and the address on legal agreements.

A state audit is often less about obscure legal doctrines and more about contradictions. If your documents tell five different stories about where you live, the state will choose the story that generates tax.

The net proceeds mindset: treat state tax like a real line item, not an afterthought

QSBS is famous because it can remove a massive federal tax line item. State tax is infamous because it can quietly put a new massive line item right back.

The mature way to think about an exit is to treat it like a cash engineering problem:

- What is the gain that will be recognized, and in which tax year(s)?
- What is the federal treatment?
- What is the state treatment based on residency, sourcing, and conformity?
- What cash will you actually receive in those same years (considering escrows, earn-outs, installments)?

When those four pieces are modeled together, you stop being surprised. You may still dislike the outcome—nobody *likes* state tax—but you'll be choosing with full information.

And if there's one final takeaway worth tattooing onto a deal checklist, it's this: a federal QSBS win is not a complete tax plan. It's a powerful component that has to survive a second system—the state system—before it becomes real money in your pocket.

6.4 Federal Reporting and the Substantiation File

QSBS is one of those tax benefits that can be *true* and still fail at the finish line. Not because the law changed, not because you misread a rule, but because the return doesn't tell a coherent story and the backup file can't support it. The IRS doesn't audit your excitement. It audits your dates, your basis, your lots, and your math.

A clean QSBS claim has two layers:

- *Computation*: how much gain you realized, how much is eligible for exclusion under the rule set(s) that apply to your shares, and how much exclusion capacity you have left for that issuer.

- *Substantiation*: the evidence trail that shows why the shares were QSBS, when you acquired them, what you paid (or contributed), how the sale proceeds were calculated, and how the amounts landed on the return.

The tricky part is that QSBS evidence is rarely stored in one place. Some of it lives with the company. Some sits in your email. Some is buried in a broker portal. Some exists only as a cap table export generated by a vendor that didn't exist when you joined the startup. Building an audit-ready file is less about finding a "QSBS form" (there isn't one) and more about assembling a dossier that makes the numbers *inevitable*.

Start with the IRS's workflow, not your spreadsheet

The IRS cares about how transactions are reported, not how you modeled them. IRS instructions establish the mechanical workflow: transactions are generally detailed on Form 8949 and then summarized onto Schedule D; QSBS exclusions are reflected through Form 8949 coding/adjustments and referenced in Schedule D instructions.

That workflow is your reporting backbone:

- *Form 8949* is where you tell the transaction-level story: date acquired, date sold, proceeds, cost/basis, and any adjustments.
- *Schedule D* is where those transactions are rolled up into totals that feed the rest of the return.

QSBS doesn't replace this machinery. It rides on it. Practically, that means you don't "file a QSBS form." You report a stock disposition and then reflect the QSBS exclusion through the right adjustment method.

One detail that matters more than it should: QSBS is typically handled on Form 8949 using an adjustment with code "Q". If your tax preparer uses software that produces a glossy summary page but the underlying Form 8949 doesn't clearly identify the QSBS adjustment, you've created an audit conversation you didn't need.

The lot problem: one company, multiple tax stories

Founders and early employees rarely hold "one block" of stock. They hold a patchwork quilt:

- founder shares and later top-up purchases,
- early exercises and later exercises,
- RSU releases post-IPO,
- shares acquired through a stock-for-stock deal,
- secondary purchases that do *not* have the same QSBS posture as original issuance.

The IRS doesn't care that you think of it all as "my equity." It cares that each lot has its own acquisition date, basis, and potentially its own eligibility profile under the expanded 2025 framework.

This is where well-meaning simplifications break. "I sold 10,000 shares" is not specific enough. What you actually sold is "10,000 shares from these lots, acquired on these dates, with this basis, qualifying under these rules." If your CPA can't see that mapping, your QSBS claim becomes a soft target even if it's correct.

A practical habit: maintain a "lot ledger" that's boring on purpose. One row per lot. Columns for acquisition date, shares, basis, evidence link, and any special notes (reorg exchange, rollover history, restrictions, etc.). In a multi-stage exit, that ledger becomes the only sane way to avoid double-counting basis, misallocating gain, or accidentally claiming exclusion on the wrong shares.

Basis is not a number; it's an argument you have to win

Basis substantiation is essential because reporting requires proceeds and basis, and QSBS planning can depend on basis-driven limitation concepts (e.g., 10× basis cap). Put differently: QSBS can be worth millions, and the IRS is fully allowed to ask, "Prove what you paid."

Basis failures happen in predictable places:

- *Early exercise or restricted stock:* the cash left your account years ago, and the only evidence is a bank statement you no longer have.
- *Non-cash contributions:* shares issued for IP, services, or converted instruments require careful documentation to support the starting point for gain.
- *Broker basis mismatches:* 1099-B basis reporting may be incomplete, wrong, or unaware of your actual tax basis history.

The best evidence is contemporaneous and redundant: wire confirmations, canceled checks, signed exercise notices, subscription agreements, and cap table entries that match. If your basis is supported only by "the cap table says so," you're betting a lot on a document that was not designed as an IRS exhibit.

Proceeds aren't always cash: the closing statement is your friend (and sometimes your enemy)

In a simple stock sale, proceeds can be straightforward. In real exits, proceeds come with dents and fingerprints:

- escrow holdbacks,
- deal expenses paid out of proceeds,
- indemnity offsets,
- earn-outs and contingent rights,
- netting arrangements in tender offers,
- partial rollovers into buyer equity.

If your reported proceeds don't reconcile to the deal documents, the IRS will not assume your version is correct. It will assume your version is convenient.

This is why your "tax file" should include the closing statement or payout letter and any schedules that show how gross consideration became your net. Those documents are also how you avoid the classic mistake of reporting *gross* proceeds when you actually received something else, or reporting *net* proceeds when the tax law treats you as having received more.

Installments and deferred payments: the paperwork doesn't end at closing

Installment/deferred-payment structures change when and how gain is reported (and which forms are used), affecting cash planning and the evidence trail needed across multiple tax years. The tax story becomes episodic: you recognize gain as payments are received (or otherwise treated as received), and your QSBS computations may need to be applied across multiple years.

That has two operational consequences that surprise people:

- You now need a *multi-year* substantiation file. The return for year one needs to explain how you will treat later payments. Later-year returns need to tie back to the original sale terms so you don't change methods midstream.
- Your documents must track not just "what I sold," but "what I'm still owed," including amendments, offsets, and any disputes that alter payment amounts.

Deferred deals reward consistency. If your reporting posture changes year-to-year because you lost track of your own method, you're inviting a very expensive kind of attention.

K-1s and pass-throughs: when your QSBS data arrives late and incomplete

When you invest through funds, SPVs, or other pass-through entities, the QSBS reporting story becomes a relay race. You can only report what you receive, and what you receive may be summarized.

That doesn't mean you're helpless. It means you should treat the K-1 package as a starting point and request what you need to defend your position: lot-level acquisition dates, issuer identification, basis and proceeds allocations, and the entity's workpapers supporting any QSBS-related reporting.

If your investment is large enough that the QSBS benefit matters, it is reasonable to expect professional-grade reporting support from the entity. If the entity can't provide it, your risk is not theoretical—you're effectively being asked to claim a major exclusion without the underlying facts.

Recordkeeping: build a file that an auditor can understand in 20 minutes

IRS recordkeeping guidance supports an "audit-ready" standard, including maintaining records and acceptable electronic storage/reproduction procedures. That's a useful standard because it forces a practical question: if someone unfamiliar with your startup, your cap table, and your deal asked for proof tomorrow, could you produce it without a scavenger hunt?

An audit-ready QSBS file has three qualities:

- *Traceable:* every number on the return ties to a document.
- *Contemporaneous:* key documents are dated and created at or near the event.
- *Coherent:* the file tells a story in order—issuance, ownership, sale, reporting.

The goal isn't to drown in PDFs. The goal is to avoid relying on memory when memory is least reliable: years after the fact, when the company has pivoted, your email has changed, and the person who ran finance has moved on.

A practical reporting workflow that keeps errors from compounding

Here's an operational approach that tends to reduce mistakes:

1. *Freeze your cap table facts:* identify what you owned immediately before the transaction and what you disposed of (including partial sales).
2. *Map lots to disposition:* decide which lots were sold and document the identification method used.
3. *Compute gain per lot:* proceeds minus basis, with notes for any special adjustments (escrow, expenses).
4. *Apply QSBS treatment per lot:* determine which lots qualify for exclusion and under what tier/rule set, then track per-issuer limit usage.
5. *Tie to return forms:* ensure Form 8949 reflects each transaction line with the appropriate QSBS adjustment posture (including code "Q" where applicable), and ensure Schedule D matches the roll-up.
6. *Archive the workpapers:* save the computation file and supporting documents together, not scattered across inboxes.

This workflow sounds meticulous because it is. The reward is that you don't have to re-litigate the same facts every time you sell another tranche or receive another deferred payment.

Substantiation checklist (audit-ready file)

The quiet benefit of keeping a file like this is psychological: you stop treating QSBS as a fragile hope and start treating it as a claim you can defend. You know what you own, what you sold, what you paid, and how the return reflects it. If the IRS ever asks, the story isn't "trust me." It's "here are the receipts, and here is the math."

Chapter 7

Common Ways People Lose QSBS and How to Prevent Them

Most QSBS disasters do not begin at the exit table. They begin years earlier with one casual assumption, one messy stock issuance, one repurchase no one flagged, or one missing record that suddenly matters when real money is on the line. This chapter helps readers spot those quiet failure points early, so they can protect eligibility before a great outcome becomes a painful tax surprise.

7.1 Formation and Funding Mistakes That Create Hidden Problems

QSBS failures rarely feel dramatic in real time. They feel like *progress*: a quick entity choice to get moving, a "temporary" SAFE because it's faster than priced equity, a "cap table cleanup" that finally makes the spreadsheet match reality. Years later, when a buyer wires eight or nine figures and everyone suddenly becomes very serious about taxes, the same choices can read like a slow-motion own goal.

The frustrating part is that many of the formation-and-funding mistakes don't create a small penalty. They create a different *kind* of asset—equity that might be economically identical to QSBS, might even be called "founder stock" in conversation, but doesn't line up with the statute's narrow definition. And Section 1202 is not sentimental. It doesn't reward grit, early risk, or "I was here from day one." It rewards stock that was issued the right way, by the right kind of company, at the right time, under the right conditions.

The first fork in the road: your entity choice decides whether QSBS is even on the menu

One of the cleanest QSBS stories begins with a boring sentence: "The company was a domestic C corporation when the stock was issued." Many startups begin somewhere else because somewhere else is easier: an LLC for pass-through taxation, an S corporation for simplicity, or a foreign entity because a cofounder lives abroad and the paperwork feels unavoidable.

Here's the hidden cost: even if the business later becomes a C corporation and later issues stock that can qualify, the earlier "founder era" equity may not convert into QSBS the way people expect. The emotional narrative ("we built this together from nothing") is not the tax narrative ("the taxpayer acquired qualified small business stock at original issuance from a domestic C corporation").

The practical danger isn't that an LLC-first path *never* works. The danger is that it often creates multiple timelines—multiple "clocks"—and founders don't notice until exit. If you formed as an LLC, granted membership interests, maybe issued profits interests, maybe had capital accounts, and only later converted, you've created at least two stories:

- the business story (continuous, from day one), and
- the stock story (which may start only when actual C-corp stock exists and is issued in a qualifying way).

A lot of QSBS disappointment is simply the gap between those two.

If you want a simple mental model: QSBS attaches to *stock*, not to your hustle. It's not a badge you earn by being early. It's a label that attaches only if the equity was created under the right legal conditions.

The "we'll convert later" trap: timing doesn't just change paperwork, it can change your holding period

Conversion is where well-meaning founders accidentally burn time. Not because they did something wrong on purpose—because they assumed tax time works like startup time. In startups, the first year feels like ten. In tax, one day is one day, and the holding period is a stopwatch.

When a company converts into a C corporation, people often assume they can count the pre-conversion years toward the holding period for QSBS purposes. Sometimes the economics are continuous—same business, same customers, same founders. But Section 1202 is picky about *what* you held during those earlier years. If you held an LLC interest, that's not C-corp stock. When you later receive C-corp stock, the holding period for that stock may start then—not when the LLC was formed.

That's not merely a timing nuance under the newer 2025 landscape with tiered holding periods. If your result depends on whether you've crossed a 3-year, 4-year, or 5-year line, the "when did the clock start?" question stops being academic. It becomes the difference between a partial benefit and a maximal one, or between planning flexibility and none.

A good way to pressure-test your own timeline is to ask a slightly obnoxious question: *If a stranger bought my equity on the day I think my holding period started, what exactly would they be buying?* If the answer is "an LLC interest," "a SAFE," or "an option," you're in the land of "maybe," not "obviously."

Original issuance: the rule that quietly turns founder lore into taxable gain

Most QSBS heartbreak is powered by one sentence: to qualify, the stock generally has to be acquired at *original issuance*—meaning you got it from the company, not from someone else. People hear that and think it's just an anti-flipper rule, meant to stop latecomers from buying in right before an exit. It is that, but it's also a cap-table reality check.

Founders and early team members often move equity around casually in the earliest days: someone backs out, someone else steps in, a cofounder "sells" a piece to a new hire, a friend writes a check to a founder personally because the company hasn't opened a bank account yet. In human terms, these are all "early ownership." In QSBS terms, they can be radically different transactions.

If you buy stock from another shareholder—no matter how early it is, no matter how founder-ish it feels—that purchase typically doesn't meet the original issuance requirement. It's a *secondary purchase*. Economically, you now own the same stock. Tax-wise, you may have purchased something that will never be QSBS in your hands, even if it would have been QSBS in the seller's hands.

That leads to a classic, painful scenario:

> A founder sells 2% to an advisor in year one "just to make it official." Everyone treats it like founder stock. At exit, the founder's gain may be eligible for Section 1202, but the advisor's may not be—because the advisor bought from the founder, not from the company.

The fix is usually straightforward if you catch it early: have the company issue stock (or options) directly under proper approvals and documentation, rather than routing ownership through an individual. The hard part is cultural: early teams often treat the cap table like a handshake. QSBS demands receipts.

When "equity" isn't stock yet: SAFEs and notes can create phantom holding periods

Startups love SAFEs and convertible notes for the same reason people love paper plates: less cleanup in the moment. But QSBS is not impressed by instruments that are "basically equity" in conversation.

A SAFE or convertible note can represent future rights to stock, but it is not stock. The holding period for QSBS generally doesn't start when you wire money into a SAFE. It starts when you actually receive stock in a conversion. That distinction is easy to miss because, operationally, the investor feels committed from day one and may even show up on an "ownership" report. But ownership reports are not the statute.

This becomes especially thorny when the company raises multiple rounds using multiple instruments:

- Angel A buys common stock directly in January 2026.
- Angel B invests through a SAFE in January 2026, which converts in July 2027.

Two checks went in at the same time. Two investors feel equally early. But their QSBS holding periods may start eighteen months apart. Under a tiered regime, that gap isn't cosmetic—it's tax outcome.

A second twist: conversions can happen in pieces. If part of a SAFE converts in one financing and the remainder converts later (or converts into different share classes under different terms), you can end up with multiple "lots" of stock with different issuance dates. At exit, that turns into a tracking problem: you may be entitled to different exclusion percentages (or different treatment entirely) for different blocks of what you thought was "one investment."

The prevention strategy isn't "never use SAFEs." It's "treat conversion as a major tax timestamp." When stock arrives, capture the details the way you'd capture a wire confirmation: date, number of shares, class of shares, and the document trail proving it was issued by the company.

Options: the most common misunderstanding is also the most expensive one

Options are a second factory for accidental phantom holding periods. People assume the holding period begins when the option is granted, because that's when they feel they "earned" the equity. But an option grant is a right to buy stock later. QSBS is about the stock itself. If the stock doesn't exist in your hands yet, the clock usually hasn't started.

That misunderstanding tends to explode in two cases:

- *Late exercise before exit.* An employee waits to exercise until an acquisition is announced. They may now own stock for weeks or months, not years. Even if the company is a perfect QSBS issuer, the employee's holding period may be far too short to capture the best result.
- *Early exercise without paperwork hygiene.* Someone early-exercises options (or believes they did), but the company never properly issued the shares, never countersigned the exercise, never updated the cap table accurately, or never filed/retained key supporting documents. Years later, the company says, "We think you exercised in 2019," and the buyer's diligence team says, "Prove it." If you can't prove it, you may not get to count it.

The emotional version of early exercise is "I took a risk." The QSBS version is "I acquired stock through a documented original issuance on a specific date." Those are not the same sentence, and your tax result will follow the second one.

"I paid for it with services" can be QSBS—but the mechanics must be clean

Founders and early employees often receive stock in exchange for services rather than cash. That can still qualify, but only if the issuance is done properly: board approval, issuance at a supportable fair market value, purchase/issuance agreements, and the right tax filings where relevant.

The hidden QSBS problem isn't "services are disallowed." It's that service-based issuances are where companies get casual: they backdate, they forget to document consideration, they skip valuation work, they issue shares before the corporation exists, or they treat a promise as an issuance.

If you want one hard-edged rule of thumb: if the company can't answer "who received what, when, and for what consideration" without rummaging through old emails, you're manufacturing future doubt. QSBS claims don't die only from being wrong; they die from being unprovable.

Secondary cleanups: the moment you "fix the cap table" is when you can accidentally break QSBS

Cap tables age like refrigerators: you stop noticing the smell until someone visits your house.

A fast-growing startup eventually reaches the moment when it has to professionalize: formal stock plans, cleaned-up vesting schedules, repurchase agreements, founder departures, option cancellations, equity grants that were promised but never issued. The instinct is to "clean things up" by transferring shares around—especially if the company is trying to avoid issuing new shares due to dilution concerns.

That can be a QSBS landmine because a "cleanup" often involves secondary transfers:

- Founder A transfers shares to Founder B to reflect a new split.
- Early advisor "assigns" stock to a new entity for estate planning.
- A departed cofounder sells shares back to another founder instead of the company repurchasing.

Some transfers may be permitted under other rules or may have their own tax treatment, but they don't automatically preserve QSBS character for the recipient. The original issuance requirement doesn't care that the transfer is fair or that it reflects the real business deal. It cares about who issued the stock to whom.

Often, the cleaner approach is not "move stock between people," but "have the corporation issue or repurchase stock in a way that maintains original issuance where needed." Yes, that can mean more corporate formalities. But formalities are cheap compared to lost tax benefits.

Entity and issuance details that matter more than people expect

A few formation-era facts are so fundamental that, if they're wrong, a later "QSBS analysis" becomes an exercise in creative writing.

Domestic C corporation status. The issuer generally needs to be a domestic C corporation. If the company is an S corporation at the time of issuance, or an LLC, or a foreign corporation, the stock issued in that period generally won't be QSBS just because the business later becomes eligible.

Gross assets at issuance. The gross-assets test is checked at issuance. A later valuation spike doesn't retroactively disqualify already-issued QSBS, but issuing stock after the company has crossed the statutory threshold can mean that *new* shares are not QSBS even if older shares are. That turns a "one cap table" story into multiple tranches with different tax character.

Class and rights changes. Recapitalizations, stock splits, and conversions can be neutral in some circumstances, but they can also create confusion about what was actually issued and when. If your cap table shows "Common (Post-Recap)" with no clean bridge to the pre-recap issuance records, you're betting your tax outcome on the hope that no one asks hard questions later.

The theme here isn't paranoia. It's precision. QSBS is generous, but it's not forgiving.

A founder-focused reality check: "I was early" is not a statutory requirement

Founders tend to describe their stake with origin stories: "We incorporated in my apartment." "I quit my job for this." "I was the first engineer." Those details matter to your identity and maybe your negotiating leverage, but Section 1202 cares about a different set of facts:

- Did the company issue stock directly to you, or did you buy it from someone else?
- Was the issuer a qualifying corporation at the time?
- Can you prove the issuance date and consideration?
- Did you actually receive stock when you think you did, or did you receive a promise to receive stock later?

If this feels harsh, it's because QSBS is a tax benefit designed to be administered by rules, not vibes. The IRS can't audit your sacrifice. It can audit documents.

A quick set of questions to ask before any early equity move

Before any formation choice, conversion, early grant, SAFE, note, or cap table adjustment, the goal is to force clarity on the handful of points that create irreversible outcomes.

Ask these questions in plain language, and insist on plain-language answers:

1. *What exactly is being issued or transferred?* Stock? An option? A SAFE? An LLC interest? A promise?
2. *Who is the issuer?* The company issuing equity, or an individual selling/transferring what they already own?
3. *What date will appear as the issuance date in corporate records?* Not the handshake date—the date reflected in board approvals, stock ledgers, and signed agreements.
4. *What starts the holding period?* The grant date, the exercise date, the conversion date, or the purchase date? If the answer is "grant," ask how you acquired *stock* on that date.
5. *Is the company a domestic C corporation right now?* If not, is the plan to become one soon, and what equity exists before that change?
6. *Will this create multiple tranches?* If you're issuing stock in multiple rounds, or converting multiple SAFEs at different times, can your cap table track issuance dates by lot?
7. *If a future buyer's diligence team asked for proof, what document would you hand them?* If the answer is "an email thread," treat that as a flashing warning light.

These questions aren't meant to turn founders into tax lawyers. They're meant to prevent the most common early-stage mistake: confusing a business deal with the legal and tax mechanics that make the deal *count*.

The most valuable habit: treat equity events like product launches

Teams that do QSBS well tend to share one boring superpower: they operationalize equity. They don't treat it as a one-time legal project. They treat it as a recurring process with checklists and sign-offs.

A simple practice makes an outsized difference: any time something happens that changes who owns what—incorporation, conversion, founder issuance, option grants, exercises, SAFE conversions, note conversions—someone creates a small "support packet" immediately. Not a 30-page memo. Just enough to pin down the facts while they're fresh: the executed documents, board approvals, cap table before and after, and the exact date the stock was issued.

That habit does two things at once. It reduces the chance you accidentally structure something as a secondary transfer. And it preserves the evidence you'll need when the stakes are no longer theoretical.

The punchline is that QSBS is often lost by people who were "basically eligible," "pretty sure it qualifies," and "definitely early." It's kept by people who can answer, years later and without drama: *Here's the stock. Here's how it was issued. Here's when the clock started.*

7.2 Operational Drift, Redemptions, and Midstream Tainting Events

The cleanest QSBS stories don't end with a clever tax move. They end with a company that simply *didn't accidentally sabotage itself.* That sounds underwhelming until you realize how many "sabotage" events are framed internally as employee-friendly, founder-friendly, or just basic housekeeping. A repurchase to tidy up the cap table. A tender offer to reduce pressure on compensation. A strategic pivot to chase revenue. A big cash balance because fundraising went well and the market got weird. None of those are villain behavior. They're normal. They're also the exact moments when QSBS can quietly stop being a sure thing.

Two forces drive most midstream QSBS damage:

- *Redemptions and repurchases* that trip the anti-abuse rules—often without anyone realizing the rules apply to a "small" transaction.

- *Operational drift* that gradually moves the company away from what Section 1202 expects during *substantially all* of the shareholder's holding period.

What makes these risks dangerous is not complexity. It's timing and memory. The events happen when the company is busy building, hiring, fundraising, shipping, and surviving. The QSBS consequences show up when the company is suddenly being measured, audited, diligence-reviewed, and priced.

Redemptions: the most expensive "routine" transaction on the cap table

A redemption is the company buying its own stock back—whether it's called a repurchase, a buyback, a company call right, a departure repurchase, or a tender offer. Everyone recognizes the economic effect (cash out, shares disappear). Fewer people recognize the QSBS effect: redemptions can disqualify stock under rules that look backward and forward in time around an issuance.

The regulation that governs this is 26 CFR §1.1202-2, and it's built like a perimeter fence. The fence isn't only around the exit. It's around the *issuance* of stock that's intended to be QSBS. That means a redemption can be a problem even when the company is healthy and the stock being redeemed has nothing to do with the stock you're worried about.

Two categories matter most in practice:

1. *Repurchases from the taxpayer (or related persons) near the issuance.* Stock generally is not QSBS if the corporation purchases more than a de minimis amount of stock from the taxpayer (or related persons) during the 4-year testing window that begins 2 years before the issuance.
2. *Significant redemptions by the corporation near the issuance.* A separate "significant redemptions" rule can disqualify stock if the

corporation makes repurchases exceeding de minimis thresholds during the 2-year window that begins 1 year before issuance, and the repurchases exceed 5% of total value over the period.

Even the phrase "testing window" should change how you think about buybacks. The question isn't only, "Did we buy stock back?" It's, "Did we buy stock back within the wrong time window relative to a tranche of QSBS stock being issued?"

That's why redemptions are such a nasty surprise in growth-stage companies: they tend to cluster around the same time as financings. Departing founder? Clean it up before the round. Employee liquidity pressure? Offer a tender alongside the round. Investor asks for a recap? It happens around the round. The round itself is often when the company issues fresh stock that everyone hopes will qualify. That proximity is exactly what the rules scrutinize.

The "departing founder repurchase" problem: one small fire, a lot of smoke

A common scene: a founder leaves. The company repurchases some vested shares under the repurchase right in the founder's restricted stock agreement. Internally, it's treated as normal governance—maybe even as a morale win ("no deadweight on the cap table").

Now add the next scene: a new priced financing closes. The company issues preferred stock to new investors and maybe common stock to some insiders. People talk about the round as creating QSBS for the new money and extending QSBS upside for early holders.

Here's where the trap lies: the repurchase can fall inside one of those QSBS testing windows surrounding the new issuance. It doesn't matter that the repurchase was "small" compared to the company's market cap, or that it was driven by a contractual right. If it crosses the regulatory thresholds, it can taint the newly issued stock—precisely the stock your newest shareholders are counting on.

The painful social dynamic is that the people most affected by this risk are often the least involved in the decision. The repurchase is negotiated by founders, HR, and counsel. The stock that could be disqualified belongs to investors who show up later, or to employees whose equity is issued later, or to founders in a later refresh grant. QSBS problems have a habit of punishing the wrong person.

Tender offers and liquidity programs: generous intent, complicated consequences

A tender offer—company-sponsored liquidity for employees and early holders—often gets framed as a maturity milestone. "We're taking care of the people who took early risk." It can also be a QSBS tripwire when it creates a pattern of repurchases that looks "significant" under the regulation.

The intuition many teams have is: "If we're just letting people sell a bit, that shouldn't impact anything." Section 1202 doesn't evaluate intent; it evaluates what happened and when. A tender can create exactly the kind of repurchase activity that triggers the significant redemptions rule if it's large enough relative to total value, and it's in the right (wrong) window around issuance.

This becomes especially thorny when tender activity and financings become a rhythm:

- Tender offer to relieve employee pressure.
- A few months later, a new round closes and issues fresh shares.
- Another tender offer is discussed as a recruiting/retention tool.

That rhythm can unintentionally layer redemptions into the windows that matter for multiple tranches. It's not that tenders are forbidden. It's that tenders require a QSBS-aware calendar and a QSBS-aware threshold check. Otherwise, the company does something that looks like good culture and discovers, at exit, that it was also quiet tax damage.

Why "de minimis" is not a comfort word

The regulation uses de minimis thresholds, including both a dollar threshold and a percentage threshold (for example, thresholds like "more than $10,000 and more than 2%" appear in the described tests). Many people see the word de minimis and mentally file it under "ignore unless we're doing something huge."

That's a mistake because early-stage and mid-stage companies are full of transactions that are small in absolute dollars but large in percentage terms. A $50,000 repurchase can be nothing for a later unicorn and very much *not nothing* for a company with a modest valuation. The math isn't aligned with your intuitive sense of what's "material."

A practical way to stay honest is to stop using only dollar-based gut checks. Ask, "What percentage of outstanding value or shares does this represent over the testing period?" Then remember the testing period is not a single day; it's a span.

Exceptions exist, but they aren't magic words

26 CFR §1.1202-2 includes specific exceptions—repurchases incident to termination of services, death, disability, divorce—that can prevent accidental tainting. Those exceptions are lifesavers when the facts fit. The danger is treating the exception label as a spell: "This is a termination repurchase, so we're fine."

In practice, exceptions are detail-sensitive. The repurchase has to be structured and documented so it actually falls within the exception. That means timing, amounts, and purpose matter, and it means counsel needs the full context—especially if there are multiple repurchases, not just one.

If you want the right posture: assume an exception is a tool you can use *after* you've mapped the transaction against the QSBS windows and thresholds, not a shortcut you apply *before* doing that work.

The operational drift problem: QSBS isn't a "day of issuance" exam

A lot of tax planning is snapshot-based: what was true on the date you signed, the date you sold, the date you filed. Section 1202 has a more annoying personality. The active business requirement in §1202(e) is tested during *substantially all* of the shareholder's holding period. That phrase is where drift lives.

Drift doesn't look like a decision. It looks like a series of reasonable moves that gradually change what the company *is*.

Three flavors show up often.

Drift #1: The balance sheet turns into a parked car full of cash

Fundraising success can create a strange tax risk: a company that's too liquid. Teams raise more than expected, or they raise at the top of the market and then slow hiring to extend runway. Suddenly the balance sheet holds a large amount of cash and investment assets.

There's a normal, healthy version of this: cash held for reasonable business needs—runway, hiring plans, product build, working capital. And then there's the version where the company starts to behave like a tiny investment fund attached to an operating business, simply because no one wants idle cash.

The drift is subtle:

- Treasury management becomes a mini-project.
- The company buys longer-dated securities.
- "Other income" starts to show up in financial updates.
- The operating plan shrinks but the asset pile doesn't.

The core QSBS idea is that the company should be an active operating business, not primarily holding investment assets. If the company's posture changes for long stretches—especially if it starts to look like capital preservation is the main activity—you're in the zone where a fresh QSBS review is smart.

Founders often ask, "How much cash is too much?" The frustrating answer is that it's not a single bright line you can memorize. The useful answer is: "Cash that is clearly tethered to an operating plan is easier to defend than cash that is clearly untethered." That's not just tax advice; it's documentation advice. If your board decks and budgets tell an operating story, your balance sheet is less likely to be misread.

Drift #2: A side project becomes the company

Startups pivot. Sometimes the pivot is the business. That's not a moral failing; it's the job. QSBS risk enters when the company crosses into excluded activities, or when the "active business" becomes something that the statute treats differently.

The most dangerous pivots are the ones that happen gradually because they don't trigger a big corporate event. A company starts as a product business and then, to accelerate revenue, adds a heavy services component. Then the services component becomes the primary driver of bookings. Then the organization chart reflects reality: the services org outgrows product.

From the inside, it feels like responding to customer demand. From a Section 1202 standpoint, it can move the company toward excluded service activities without anyone deliberately choosing that outcome.

The defensive habit is simple: any time revenue composition changes meaningfully—especially toward services—pause and ask whether you're changing the QSBS posture of the company during the holding period. You don't need to litigate it in your head. You just need to recognize it as a "this deserves a tax check" moment, like recognizing a strange noise in your car before you drive across the desert.

Drift #3: The company starts buying businesses (and the asset mix changes)

Acquisitions can change what the company owns and what it does. Sometimes that's the point: buy a team, buy IP, buy distribution. But acquisitions can also change asset composition in ways that make the "active business" narrative harder to tell, especially if the company starts holding subsidiaries or significant passive assets.

This risk isn't an argument against M&A. It's an argument against sleepwalking through it. If a deal changes the company's assets and activities, it should also trigger a QSBS refresh—particularly if the deal is large relative to the company.

Midstream QSBS risk management: stop relying on memory and start relying on triggers

The most successful QSBS outcomes are rarely the result of a brilliant one-time analysis. They come from a short list of triggers that automatically force the company (and key holders) to take a fresh look.

Here are triggers that deserve a QSBS-aware review because they can affect eligibility or taint specific tranches:

- Any corporate repurchase of stock (including routine departure repurchases).
- Any tender offer or structured liquidity program.
- Any investor request to "clean up" the cap table as a closing condition.
- Any major financing that issues new stock intended to qualify.

- Any significant shift in business model, especially toward services or away from the original operating plan.
- A sustained build-up of cash and investments not clearly tied to near-term operating needs.

This trigger approach has a nice side effect: it changes the internal conversation. Instead of "Are we still QSBS?"—a vague question that people avoid because it sounds legalistic—the question becomes "Did we hit a trigger?" That's a concrete operational question, which means it's more likely to be asked and answered.

Who should be in the room when these events happen

QSBS failures often happen because the decision-makers are missing one person: someone whose job is to be boring about risk. Not because anyone is careless, but because startups are optimized for speed and focus.

When a trigger hits, the minimum "QSBS-aware" group usually includes:

- *Company counsel* (because redemptions and financings are legal events, and the regulatory windows are technical).
- *Finance leadership* (because cash/investment posture and transaction sizing live here).
- *The cap table owner* (often the CFO's team, sometimes outside administrators; they control the issuance timeline and share counts).

HR often belongs in the conversation too, not because HR is responsible for QSBS, but because HR triggers a surprising number of repurchases: terminations, option cancellations, repurchase rights, and tender participation.

If that sounds like too many cooks, remember what's at stake: the same transaction can be framed as a culture win and become a tax loss. A twenty-minute pre-check with the right people is cheaper than explaining to employees why their expected tax treatment changed after the fact.

A tranche-aware mindset: the company can be "fine" and a specific issuance can still be in trouble

One mental mistake shows up constantly: people think QSBS is a single status the company either has or doesn't have. In reality, a company can be a perfectly good operating business and still have a specific *issuance* of stock that's compromised by redemptions in the relevant windows.

That's why midstream discipline matters most around financings and equity grants. Each issuance is its own moment with its own surrounding facts. The company's overall narrative might be excellent—active business, strong growth, clean governance—and the new shares can still get tangled in the redemption rules if repurchases were clustered nearby.

The operational takeaway is slightly counterintuitive: when the company is doing well and being generous with liquidity, that's when it's most likely to create redemption activity that collides with new issuances. Success creates the temptation to run programs. Programs create patterns. Patterns create testing-window problems.

A practical pre-flight checklist before any repurchase or tender

Before signing the paperwork on a buyback, repurchase, or tender, the company (and key holders) should be able to answer these questions without hand-waving:

1. *What stock is being repurchased, from whom, and are any sellers "related persons" to holders we care about?*

2. *What other repurchases happened in the surrounding period?* Not just this quarter—map the full 4-year and 2-year windows that might matter for upcoming issuances.
3. *Is the company about to issue QSBS-intended stock?* That includes financings, option exercises tied to a transaction, refresh grants, and founder issuances.
4. *Do any exceptions apply, and do the facts actually fit?* If you're relying on an exception incident to termination of services (or death, disability, divorce), make sure the structure and documentation align.
5. *Who owns the record?* Decide who is responsible for maintaining the repurchase log and linking it to issuance dates by tranche.

If the answers are fuzzy, it's not a sign to panic. It's a sign to pause. The cost of pausing is small. The cost of getting it wrong can be permanent.

The surprising upside of doing this well: it makes the company more investable

Investors like companies that don't generate unforced errors. A QSBS-aware approach to repurchases and operational drift is, in a quiet way, a governance signal. It tells investors that the company can run a financing without last-minute chaos, can execute employee programs without creating weird side effects, and can tell a coherent story during diligence.

That's the real point of midstream QSBS hygiene: it isn't legal perfection. It's keeping a valuable feature of the equity intact while the company grows. When the exit finally arrives, you want the story to be boring: the company operated like a real business, the cap table actions were deliberate, and the tax benefit that was earned on paper still exists in reality.

7.3 Documentation Gaps That Surface at Exit or Audit

A QSBS claim can die in a very unglamorous way: not with a dramatic "disqualified" memo, but with a polite request that no one can satisfy. "Can you send the stock purchase agreement?" "Do you have the board consent approving the issuance?" "What's the issuer's gross assets at the time the shares were issued?" "When exactly did you acquire the stock?" If the only honest answer is a long pause followed by "we can probably reconstruct it," you're no longer arguing tax law. You're arguing memory.

That's the uncomfortable truth: taxpayers bear the burden of proving entitlement to the exclusion. If the IRS (or a buyer's diligence team, or your own CPA preparing an aggressive return position) asks for evidence and you can't produce it, you can lose even when the underlying story is basically correct. Courts and the IRS aren't obligated to fill in missing facts with optimism, especially when timing and acquisition mechanics are central to eligibility.

Documentation failures happen for a simple reason: startups are built in sprints, while tax benefits are earned in slow motion. The moment you receive stock can be five or ten years before the moment anyone scrutinizes it. By then, the company has changed counsel, switched cap table systems, migrated cloud drives three times, and hired people who were in middle school when the first SAFE was signed. The gap is predictable. That's why it's preventable.

Proof beats confidence: the QSBS position you can defend is the one that matters

You can tell how serious a QSBS position is by how it behaves under friction. If a claim only works as long as everyone nods along—founders, finance, outside counsel, tax preparer—then it's not really a claim. It's a shared assumption.

The stakes at exit make assumptions brittle. A buyer's tax team is incentivized to find anything that reduces purchase price, increases escrow, or justifies extra diligence. Your tax preparer is incentivized to avoid signing onto a position that can't be substantiated. And the IRS, when it examines a return, has its own internal playbook for how to pull technical threads—something underscored by IRS Chief Counsel Advice, which shows how carefully the agency can analyze Section 1202 issues when facts are murky.

The best mindset shift is to treat QSBS eligibility like a warranty claim. The product may be defective or fine; either way, you only get paid if you can show the receipt, the serial number, and the date of purchase.

The "exit binder" problem: at the worst possible time, everyone asks for the same old documents

Exits create document gravity. Suddenly, every party wants the same core set of records, and they want them quickly:

- the buyer for diligence,
- the company for disclosure schedules,
- shareholders for personal tax reporting,
- and sometimes lenders or insurers if the deal structure involves escrow, RWI insurance, or post-close adjustments.

QSBS adds a special twist: it pushes diligence beyond "who owns what" into "how was it acquired" and "what was the company at that moment." That's why founders often feel blindsided. They did keep a cap table. They did have a stock plan. They did incorporate. Yet QSBS demands more granular proof than the average corporate housekeeping file.

And because Section 1202 is claimed at the shareholder level, the company's diligence file is often incomplete from the individual's perspective. The company may have records of its own actions, but not each taxpayer's basis computations, holding period nuances, and transfer history. Many people discover too late that they need their own parallel evidence file, even if the company is well-run.

The quiet villain: timing disputes and "when did you really acquire it?"

Most tax fights aren't about whether a startup is real. They're about dates.

Ownership timing can be disputed in ways that feel almost insulting. A founder might say, "I've owned these shares since we started." A document trail might say, "You signed the purchase agreement later." A settlement might say, "This agreement establishes ownership as of now." An unsigned board consent might create an opening for someone to argue the issuance never happened when you think it did.

Cases and commentary highlight that courts and the IRS can deny QSBS where facts like ownership timing and acquisition date are not adequately supported. The reason is simple: the holding period and the acquisition mechanism are not vibes-based elements. They're outcome-determinative.

Here are common real-world triggers for timing disputes:

- *Founder fallout.* A cofounder leaves and later claims they never properly received shares, or received fewer than recorded.
- *"We agreed, but we didn't paper it."* An equity promise is treated as ownership internally, but the issuance is documented months later.
- *Settlements that rewrite history.* A lawsuit or separation ends with a settlement that clarifies or reallocates shares; the legal event can become the key acquisition moment.

- *Administrative migrations.* The cap table system changes and early grants are re-entered manually, often with approximated dates.

The defense against timing disputes is not arguing harder at exit. It's creating a record at the moment the facts happen, when signatures are obtainable and memories are still accurate.

Your tax return is part of the proof

Even if your QSBS story is substantively correct, it still has to be *claimed* correctly. Claiming the Section 1202 exclusion is not just a legal conclusion; it must be reflected properly in the capital gains reporting workflow—Schedule D and typically Form 8949. That means your return mechanics and your support file are part of the risk surface.

This surprises people because they think of QSBS as a "yes/no" election. It's not. It's a reporting position embedded inside a capital gains computation that may include multiple lots, multiple issuance dates, multiple sale tranches, or rollover and withholding items depending on the transaction.

A weak return position isn't always "wrong," but it is often "inviting questions." If an IRS examiner sees a large capital gain with a large adjustment and thin documentation, the path of least resistance is to ask for substantiation. If you can't respond quickly and coherently, the examiner doesn't need to prove you're wrong—you need to prove you're right.

The core QSBS evidence file: documents that answer five blunt questions

QSBS documentation can be reduced to five blunt questions. If you can answer these with contemporaneous records, you're usually in good shape:

1. *Who received what?*
2. *From whom?* (the corporation at original issuance versus another holder)
3. *When?*
4. *For what consideration?* (cash, services, conversion)
5. *Why was the company still eligible at that moment?* (corporate status, gross assets, business activity posture)

Notice what's missing: opinions. A QSBS claim is not defended by "our lawyer said it should qualify" or "everyone in the round expected it." Those may be helpful context, but the spine of the defense is documentary evidence that pins down facts.

Below are the most important categories of records to retain, with the "why" attached so the list doesn't become another boring compliance checklist.

Incorporation and tax status evidence: prove the issuer was the right kind of company

Keep:

- certificate/articles of incorporation and any amendments,
- evidence of the company's tax classification as a C corporation when relevant issuances occurred,
- any conversion documents if the company changed entity form.

Why it matters: if the company wasn't the right kind of issuer at the time stock was acquired, none of the later heroics matter. And at exit, people often conflate "we were always a startup" with "we were always a qualifying corporation." The documents prevent that confusion from becoming a tax problem.

Board approvals and consents: prove the company actually authorized the issuance

Keep:

- board minutes or written consents approving stock issuances, option grants, plan adoptions, and material amendments,
- stock plan documents and adoption approvals,
- approvals for SAFE/note forms and financing closings where conversions occur.

Why it matters: authorization is the company's "receipt." If shares appear on a cap table without a corresponding approval trail, you've created an evidentiary gap that gets ugly under scrutiny. This becomes especially sensitive for early issuances when governance is informal and signatures are harder to reconstruct later.

Stock purchase agreements and subscription documents: prove original issuance and consideration

Keep:

- stock purchase agreements (founder issuances, early employee issuances, investor subscriptions),
- subscription agreements or closing binders for priced rounds,
- evidence of payment (wire confirmations, canceled checks) or service consideration documentation.

Why it matters: original issuance is a fact pattern, not a label. These documents show the stock came from the corporation and identify the consideration paid, which is crucial both for eligibility and for basis. If you can't prove consideration, you may end up with basis questions at the exact moment you want basis to be boring.

Option and restricted stock paperwork: prove the stock exists when you think it does

Keep:

- option grant notices and the underlying plan terms,
- exercise notices and proof of exercise consideration (cashless exercise mechanics, net exercise details, or cash payment evidence),
- restricted stock purchase agreements, vesting schedules, and repurchase right documents.

Why it matters: many QSBS holding-period arguments turn into "grant versus exercise versus vesting" confusion. A clean file makes the timeline hard to dispute. A messy file turns a straightforward timeline into a debate.

Also, keep records of any modifications—repricings, cancellations, extensions, or early exercises—because those are the moments when "what did you actually hold?" becomes a real question rather than a theoretical one.

SAFE and note conversion records: prove when stock was actually issued

Keep:

- the executed SAFE/note instruments,
- conversion agreements or conversion notices,
- cap table snapshots immediately before and after conversion,
- the financing closing binder that triggered conversion.

Why it matters: conversions create stock, and the stock's issuance date can be the hinge for holding period and tiered outcomes. Conversions are also where companies tend to rely on cap table platforms without preserving the underlying documents. Platforms are helpful, but they are not evidence by themselves if you can't export and explain the underlying transaction.

Cap table history: not the current cap table, the *time machine*

Keep:

- periodic cap table exports (at least at every financing, major issuance, redemption, and recap),
- transaction ledgers showing issuances, transfers, cancellations, and repurchases.

Why it matters: at exit, you're rarely proving one static fact. You're proving a history. A current cap table is a snapshot; the IRS and diligence teams often want the movie. If you can produce clean snapshots across time, you reduce the risk that someone treats your ownership history as a reconstruction exercise.

A surprisingly common failure is having a pristine current cap table but no historical artifacts. That's like having a bank balance but no statements. It's not persuasive when someone challenges a date.

Gross-assets support at issuance: the eligibility fact that gets forgotten because it isn't exciting

Keep:

- balance sheet or trial balance around issuance dates,
- valuation workpapers used for accounting or investor reporting,
- any internal computations showing how gross assets were determined when stock was issued.

Why it matters: this is one of those facts that can be true and still hard to prove later. People remember the round price and the post-money valuation; they don't remember what the company's gross assets were for QSBS purposes at the issuance moment. If a tranche's eligibility depends on being under the threshold at issuance, you want the ability to show the math without guesswork.

Redemption and repurchase logs: prove what happened in the windows that matter

Keep:

- a repurchase ledger showing date, seller, number of shares, class, and consideration,
- tender offer documents and participation summaries,
- any board approvals related to repurchase programs.

Why it matters: as discussed with midstream tainting risk, small repurchases can have outsize consequences depending on timing windows. If you can't reconstruct repurchases reliably, you can't confidently analyze whether a disqualifying redemption pattern occurred around key issuance dates.

This is also where startup "informality" causes needless damage: repurchases are sometimes recorded inconsistently because they're scattered across HR files, legal docs, and accounting entries. One unified log makes later analysis possible without heroics.

Business-activity evidence: tell a consistent story about what the company did during the holding period

Keep:

- board decks and investor updates that describe the operating business,
- revenue mix summaries (especially if services become meaningful),

- documentation of how cash was intended to be used (budgets, hiring plans), particularly when cash balances are large.

Why it matters: Section 1202's "substantially all" concept makes the operating story part of the evidence. You don't need a novel; you need contemporaneous artifacts that show the company was running an active business and that its assets and activities weren't drifting into a different posture.

The subtle advantage: good operating documentation already exists in most healthy companies. The QSBS move is simply to preserve it in a way that remains accessible after staff turnover and system migrations.

The most common QSBS documentation myths (and why they're dangerous)

Myth: "The cap table is the proof." The cap table is a summary. Summaries are only as good as the underlying documents. When challenged, a cap table without agreements and approvals is like a spreadsheet that claims you own a house without a deed.

Myth: "Our lawyers have it." Maybe. Maybe not. Law firms change, files get archived, portals expire, and responsibility is diffuse. Even when counsel has the documents, extracting them during a rushed exit can be painful and expensive. You want your own copy of your own key papers.

Myth: "We can recreate it from emails." Email reconstruction is how good tax outcomes turn into mediocre settlements. Email trails are messy, incomplete, and often ambiguous about the exact action taken. They're supporting actors, not the lead.

A practical system: keep a "QSBS support packet" for every equity event

The easiest way to make documentation real is to shrink the scope. Don't try to build a perfect archive for the entire company overnight. Instead, treat every equity event as something that produces a small packet—five to fifteen documents—that answers the blunt questions.

For an issuance, the packet might include:

- board consent approving the issuance,
- the executed purchase/subscription agreement,
- proof of payment or service consideration documentation,
- a cap table export before/after,
- the company balance sheet around the issuance date.

For a conversion, add the instrument and conversion documentation. For a repurchase, add the repurchase agreement, approval, and update to the repurchase log.

The point is not to hoard PDFs. The point is to create a chain of evidence that a stranger can follow without needing your personal memory to interpret it.

When the company is cooperative and when it isn't

Founders and employees often assume the company will help at exit. Usually it will, but "will" and "can" are different words. Companies in an acquisition are busy. Finance teams are overwhelmed. Legal teams are negotiating disclosures. Your request for "a copy of my 2018 restricted stock agreement and the board minutes approving it" can drop to the bottom of the pile, not out of malice but out of triage.

If the company becomes uncooperative—because of a dispute, a layoff, a shutdown, or just chaos—your personal QSBS position shouldn't depend on being able to persuade someone to dig through an archive.

That's why each shareholder who expects a meaningful Section 1202 result should keep their own file containing:

- their executed agreements,
- their proof of payment,
- their exercise and conversion records,
- and periodic cap table snapshots showing their holdings.

It's not mistrust. It's self-respect.

The best time to fix documentation is when it feels unnecessary

Documentation work is hardest when it's urgent. It's easiest when it feels optional.

The moment right after a financing closes—when the documents are already compiled and signatures are fresh—is the moment to save what you'll need later. The moment right after an exercise—when you have the notice, the payment evidence, and the updated cap table—is the moment to archive. The moment right after a repurchase—when everyone remembers why it happened and how it was structured—is the moment to update the repurchase log.

The alternative is doing it at exit, when every missing piece becomes a negotiation: between your tax preparer and their risk tolerance, between the company's legal team and their bandwidth, between the buyer's diligence team and their skepticism.

A QSBS claim is a high-value position made of low-status work: PDFs, signatures, timestamps, and spreadsheets. Keep the low-status work clean, and the high-value outcome is much harder to take away.

7.4 A Practical QSBS Decision Framework for Confident Action

QSBS decisions rarely announce themselves with a banner that says "Tax Moment." They show up disguised as ordinary startup life: a SAFE conversion that happens automatically at a closing, a departing founder whose shares get repurchased on the way out, an employee who wants to exercise before a tender, an investor who asks for a quick secondary sale to cover a mortgage. Each event feels local and solvable. The QSBS consequence is global and permanent.

The goal is not to turn every board meeting into a tax seminar. The goal is to build a reflex: when an equity event is about to happen, run a short set of checkpoints that tell you whether you're in a green zone (proceed), a yellow zone (proceed, but document and confirm), or a red zone (stop and get specialist review before you do something irreversible). Think of it as change-control for one of the company's most valuable invisible assets.

A good framework does two things at once. First, it protects eligibility—by catching the handful of issues that most often break Section 1202. Second, it protects *your future self*—by forcing you to capture evidence and calculations while the facts are still fresh enough to be proved.

Checkpoint 0: Regime determination (the rulebook depends on when each tranche was acquired)

The first question is deceptively simple: *Which version of Section 1202 applies to this specific block of stock?* After the OBBBA changes, regime determination matters in a way that catches even sophisticated teams off guard. Many companies now have "mixed-era" equity: one holder may own multiple lots of the same issuer's stock, acquired on different dates, under different rules.

This is where otherwise smart people make an expensive shortcut: they apply the new rules to everything because the company is "post-2025," or they apply the old rules to everything because the company "started before 2025." Neither approach matches how the statute works in practice. The relevant unit is the *acquisition/issuance date of the stock in the holder's hands*. That's why tranche-by-tranche tracking isn't administrative fussiness—it's how you avoid applying the wrong benefit to the wrong shares on a tax return.

A simple operational fix: maintain a holder-level ledger that shows, for each lot, the date acquired, how acquired (original issuance, exercise, conversion), and the regime you believe applies. When a new issuance happens, the ledger gets a new line item. When a conversion happens, it creates stock lots with their own timestamps. When a recap happens, you preserve the bridge from old to new so dates don't dissolve into "sometime in 2019."

Checkpoint 1: Issuer eligibility and business alignment (is the company still the right kind of engine?)

You already know the "what" of issuer eligibility; the practical question is *when* to re-check it. The answer is: any time the company's behavior changes in a way that would look different to an outsider reading the financials, not just the pitch deck.

Green-zone facts usually look boring:

- The company is plainly operating an active business.
- Cash and investments tell an operating story (runway, hiring plan, build plan), not a "we parked money for years" story.
- The company hasn't drifted toward excluded service activities as a main identity.

Yellow-zone facts look like success creating new posture:

- The company has accumulated a very large cash balance relative to near-term operating needs.

- Revenue has tilted toward services or advising because it's easier to sell, even if product remains the brand.
- The company has begun acquiring other businesses or holding assets that complicate the "active business" narrative.

Red-zone facts are when the company begins to resemble something Section 1202 didn't intend to subsidize:

- The business model has effectively become an excluded activity (or is trending there) for meaningful stretches of time.
- A large portion of assets are not clearly tied to operating needs for a sustained period.

The action step is not "panic and stop operating." It's "force a fresh analysis, then preserve the output." A short memo, an internal worksheet, or counsel's email that ties the facts to the statutory tests becomes extremely valuable later—especially when the people making today's decisions are no longer at the company.

Checkpoint 2: Acquisition mechanics (did you actually acquire stock in a qualifying way, on the date you think you did?)

This checkpoint prevents the most common category error in startup equity: treating "economic ownership" as the same thing as "stock acquired at original issuance." Under Section 1202, how you acquired the stock is often more important than how early you got involved.

Green-zone acquisition mechanics:

- Stock purchased directly from the company under a signed agreement with board approval and proof of payment.
- Stock received on an exercise that is properly documented, countersigned, paid for, and reflected in the cap table and stock ledger.

- Stock received upon conversion of a SAFE or note, with executed conversion documentation and clear issuance records.

Yellow-zone mechanics (often fixable with cleanup and documentation):

- Paperwork exists, but dates are inconsistent across the cap table, agreements, and approvals.
- A conversion or exercise happened "administratively," but the supporting documents are scattered across systems or incomplete.
- A secondary transfer happened for innocent reasons (cap table cleanup, founder re-split), and you're assuming QSBS character transfers neatly.

Red-zone mechanics:

- You acquired shares by buying from another holder and are treating them as QSBS in your hands without analysis.
- You believe you "owned" shares for years, but the first executed documents establishing ownership are much later (often surfaced in a dispute or settlement).
- The company cannot produce approvals or issuance documents, leaving the acquisition date effectively unprovable.

The action step here is straightforward: when the acquisition path is anything other than a clean issuance with clean documents, take the extra step to confirm the tax story before you lock in the structure. It's cheaper to re-paper a transaction now than to negotiate with an IRS examiner or a buyer's diligence team later.

Checkpoint 3: Timing reality (when does the clock start for this holder and this lot?)

Timing errors are the silent killers because they don't feel like "mistakes." They feel like optimism.

Green-zone timing:

- The stock issuance date is clear and supported, and it matches the date the holder is using for their QSBS timeline.
- The holder understands that a SAFE/note is not stock and is tracking the conversion date as the stock's start date.

Yellow-zone timing:

- There were multiple conversions or exercises at different times, creating multiple lots with different clocks.
- The company did a recap or reorganization and the holder's timeline depends on bridging old records to new shares.

Red-zone timing:

- The holder is relying on a grant date, promise date, or "we agreed" date as the start of the stock timeline.
- The holder needs a particular date to cross a threshold, but cannot prove the date with executed documents.

Timing is also where the OBBBA tiered structure makes discipline pay. When different exclusion tiers attach to different time horizons, "close enough" can be very expensive. The best practical habit is to keep a simple lot schedule that ties each issuance to a timestamp and a source document, then treat any new equity event as the creation of a new line item.

Checkpoint 4: Redemption and repurchase taint checks (26 CFR §1.1202-2 is a calendar problem, not a vibes problem)

If there is one midstream risk that deserves a procedural safeguard, it's redemptions. The regulation is technical, but your internal rule can be simple: *before issuing stock that you expect holders to treat as QSBS, check the repurchase history inside the lookback windows.*

The key facts to remember, in plain language:

- Stock generally is not QSBS if the corporation purchases more than a de minimis amount of stock from the taxpayer (or related persons) during the 4-year testing window that begins 2 years before issuance.
- A separate "significant redemptions" rule can disqualify stock if the corporation makes repurchases exceeding de minimis thresholds during the 2-year window that begins 1 year before issuance, and the repurchases exceed 5% of total value over the period.
- The thresholds include both dollar and percentage components, so "small" in dollars is not the same as "small" under the rule.

Green-zone redemption posture:

- No repurchases in the relevant windows, or repurchases clearly below thresholds, with a clean repurchase log.

Yellow-zone posture:

- Repurchases occurred (departure repurchases, small tender participation), but you can quantify them and analyze them against the regulation before issuing new QSBS-intended stock.

Red-zone posture:

- The company has repurchased shares, but cannot reconstruct the history reliably.
- A large tender or repurchase program occurred close to an issuance, and no one did a taint analysis at the time.
- You are relying on an exception (termination of services, death, disability, divorce) without confirming the transaction actually fits the exception's requirements.

The action step is not "never repurchase shares." It's "treat repurchases as regulated events that require a dated analysis and a preserved log." Once you implement that discipline, the regulation becomes manageable: you're no longer guessing; you're measuring.

Checkpoint 5: Documentation and reporting readiness (can you prove it on Schedule D and Form 8949?)

QSBS is claimed on a tax return, not in a pitch deck. Claiming the Section 1202 exclusion is not just a legal conclusion; it must be reflected properly in the capital gains reporting workflow (Schedule D and typically Form 8949). That means you need two things: (1) correct computation, lot by lot, and (2) a support file that makes the computation defensible.

Green-zone readiness:

- You have executed agreements, approvals, conversion/exercise records, cap table history, and gross-assets support at issuance.
- You can map each lot sold to its acquisition date, basis, and regime.

Yellow-zone readiness:

- Documents exist, but they're scattered across portals and inboxes; you can assemble them, but it will take time.

- The company can produce records, but you as the shareholder have not retained your own copies.

Red-zone readiness:

- Your position depends on reconstructing key facts from emails or unsigned drafts.
- You cannot tie the shares sold to a clean issuance record and basis computation.

A useful trick: before a sale closes, draft a one-page "lot schedule" for your own holdings. Not a memo full of conclusions—just a table: lot, acquisition date, acquisition method, shares, basis, regime, and where the proof lives. If you can't fill in a cell without guessing, you've found your real risk.

Checkpoint 6: Exclusion capacity (eligibility is only half the game)

Even perfectly qualifying stock doesn't give unlimited exclusion. The per-issuer limitation means you need to know how much exclusion capacity you can actually use for that issuer, including any prior exclusions already claimed for stock of the same company.

This is the checkpoint that turns "QSBS eligible" into "QSBS optimized." It's also the checkpoint that prevents an unpleasant surprise when a taxpayer assumes all gain is excluded and later learns that only part of it fits within the cap structure.

Green-zone capacity planning:

- You track cumulative excluded gain per issuer and understand whether you are using a dollar cap, a multiple-of-basis cap, or a combination depending on the regime and facts.

Yellow-zone:

- You are eligible but haven't modeled the per-issuer limitation; you need a computation before signing the return position.

Red-zone:

- You have multiple trusts, gifts, or transfers and no consolidated tracking of how much exclusion has already been "used" for this issuer across related planning.

The action step is to build a simple tracker that survives turnover and time. A spreadsheet is fine. What matters is that it's updated every time you sell, gift, or otherwise dispose of stock in a way that could affect the issuer-level tally.

Checkpoint 7: Mitigation paths (if you must sell early, route the decision deliberately)

Sometimes the clean QSBS move is—not available. Life happens. A founder gets divorced. An angel needs liquidity. An employee can't carry the tax cost of exercising and holding. A buyer offers an early partial cash-out with a deadline.

When a sale happens before the relevant time thresholds, you still want a deliberate path rather than an accidental one. For early liquidity needs or forced sales before meeting the relevant holding period, Section 1045 rollover may be a mitigation lever, but it is time-sensitive and process-heavy. The point isn't that every early sale should roll. The point is that an early sale should trigger a conscious evaluation of mitigation options while they are still available.

This is where the framework earns its keep: it routes a stressful personal decision into an orderly checklist—regime, acquisition facts, timing, documentation, and mitigation feasibility—so you don't discover options only after the window to use them has closed.

How to use the framework without becoming the "tax person"

The healthiest way to operationalize this is to assign ownership of the checkpoints based on where the facts naturally live:

- Legal owns authorization, issuance mechanics, and the repurchase calendar.
- Finance owns gross-assets support, cash posture narratives, and transaction logs.
- The cap table administrator owns lot-level history and exports.
- Individual holders own their personal support files and basis records.

Then pick the moments when the framework automatically runs: financings, repurchases, tenders, conversions, recapitalizations, reorganizations, and meaningful business-model shifts. Treat those as QSBS change-control moments, not because QSBS should dominate the company's priorities, but because those events are exactly when small paperwork choices become large tax outcomes.

www.ingramcontent.com/pod-product-compliance
Lightning Source LLC
LaVergne TN
LVHW010714061126
851857LV00014B/1185